GET DIVORCED WITHOUT GETTING SCREWED

A MAN'S STRATEGIC GUIDE TO WINNING BEFORE, DURING, AND AFTER DIVORCE

JOHN NACHLINGER

Copyright © 2026 John Nachlinger
All rights reserved.

No part of this book may be reproduced, stored in a retrieval system, or transmitted in any form or by any means, electronic, mechanical, photocopying, recording, or otherwise, without prior written permission of the publisher, except for brief quotations in reviews.

This book is provided for informational and educational purposes only. It is not intended as, and should not be interpreted as, legal advice. The use of this book does not establish an attorney-client relationship. Laws and legal outcomes differ by jurisdiction and individual circumstances, and readers are encouraged to consult a qualified attorney regarding their specific situation.

First Edition

Published by Divorce Shield Press

ISBN: 9798993814919

Library of Congress Control Number: 2025927358

Printed in the United States of America

*For my daughter Sydney and husband Rafael.
My life is better because you both keep me
on my toes and ensure there is never a dull moment.*

This book offers strategic guidance informed by the author's decades of experience and thousands of cases. However, every situation is different. Use this information to prepare yourself but always consult a qualified attorney in your area about your specific circumstances. Nothing in this book constitutes legal advice for your particular case.

CONTENTS

Introduction	vii
Emergency Quick-Start Guide	xv

PART ONE
THE WAKE-UP CALL

1. When Good Men Get Blindsided	3
2. Recognizing the Point of No Return	13

PART TWO
THE PREPARATION PHASE

3. The Four Pillars of Divorce Preparation	25
4. Building Your Divorce Team	39

PART THREE
THE BATTLE PHASE

5. Avoiding the Early Execution Errors	53
6. The Mediation vs. Litigation Decision	67
7. When Divorce Stays Civil	75
8. Mastering the Custody Chess Game	83
9. Surviving High-Conflict Divorce	91
10. Financial Warfare and Asset Protection	103
11. What Your Wife's Attorney Is Telling Her	111

PART FOUR
THE RESOLUTION PHASE

12. Negotiating from Strength, Not Desperation	121
13. Divorce-Proofing Your Agreement	131
14. Making Your Agreement Work Long-Term	139

PART FIVE
THE PHOENIX PHASE

15. Surviving the First Year	151
16. Stabilizing Your New Life	167
17. Thriving in Your 2.0 Life	183
18. Building Long-Term Wealth as a Divorced Man	193

19. Conclusion 203

APPENDICES

Appendix A: Divorce Document Checklist 211
Appendix B: State-Specific Divorce Resources 215
Appendix C: Sample Parenting Plans That Work 219
Appendix D: Financial Recovery Roadmap 223
Appendix E: The Divorce Shield Method Quick Reference 229

INTRODUCTION

THE $375,000 MISTAKE

 "I'm being a good husband," George Allen thought, as he moved out of the family home.

They weren't divorced yet, but his wife was always upset, their kids seemed stressed by the constant fighting, and he figured giving everyone some space would help cool things down. "Just for a few weeks," he told himself, as he packed a bag for his brother's basement.

After all, a motel was an unnecessary expense. But he could've stayed at The Four Seasons for less than that single decision cost him — $375,000 — over the next eighteen months.

When George finally got to court, the judge looked at the custody arrangement that had "worked" during his six basement-dwelling months and made it permanent. George went from seeing his kids every day, to getting them every other weekend. His temporary support payments became his permanent obligations, and those other "temporary" arrangements he'd agreed to? Well, they became the cruddy foundation for everything that followed.

George's story teaches us something crucial about divorce:

Your biggest mistakes happen in the first 90 days, often before you even hire a lawyer.

Three years later, George had rebuilt his life and finances. Today, he runs a successful consulting business, has a strong relationship with his kids despite their limited time together, and got remarried to a woman who understands what he's been through. That success came from learning hard lessons and applying them strategically.

Two realities about divorce stand out above all others:

1. **Bad early decisions create lasting consequences**
2. **Calculated decisions can help you recover and build something better.**

WHY MOST MEN GET BLINDSIDED

Every week, successful men walk into divorce attorneys' offices completely unprepared. And they're not stupid — for the most part — they're engineers, business owners, teachers, and executives who handle complex problems at work every day. But when it comes to their divorces… they make amateur-hour mistakes that cost them dearly.

They trust their wife's promises to "keep things fair." They move out of the house to "give them space." They agree to temporary custody schedules that become permanent. They hand over financial control because they feel guilty about the marriage ending.

Meanwhile, their wives have often been preparing for months, guided by attorneys who understand exactly how the system works, and work it in their favor.

The playing field isn't level. But that doesn't mean you have to lose.

THE FOUR PILLARS THAT CHANGE EVERYTHING

After guiding over 2,000 families through divorce over twenty-three years, I've learned a thing or two about two not being an even number.

So, why do so many get screwed?

Nope. It isn't luck, money, or having a better lawyer.

The difference is careful planning, using what I call the Four Pillars Framework:

Pillar 1: Protect Your Money - understand how assets get divided, how support gets calculated, and the moves you can make to protect your financial future.

Pillar 2: Protect Your Children - document your relationship with your kids to build the evidence that wins equal custody.

Pillar 3: Protect Your Freedom - avoid false allegations and stay out of legal trouble that can destroy your case.

Pillar 4: Protect Your Sanity - maintain your physical and mental health so you can make smart decisions under pressure.

Most men focus on just one pillar, ignoring the other three. That's why they fail. You need all four working together to navigate divorce successfully.

WHO AM I TO GUIDE YOU?

John Nachlinger - veteran of the divorce trenches for over two decades, at your service. While I've represented both men and women over the years, I'm a family law attorney who's seen time and time again how men consistently get worse advice and make more costly mistakes.

I started **Divorce Shield** after realizing that most divorce attorneys don't proactively help men thoroughly prepare for divorce. They're reactive. But what's done is done, and then there's only so much that can be done. By the time most men walk into a lawyer's office, they've already made the mistakes that determine their outcome.

My approach is different. I help men understand what's coming and prepare strategically for it. Over the years, I've guided thousands through divorce, helping them avoid common traps, build stronger relationships with their kids, and safeguard their financial futures.

The strategies in this book come from real cases, real outcomes, and real lessons learned from both guys who nailed their divorces.... and those who got screwed. Don't let that be you.

SUCCESS STORIES THAT PROVE STRATEGY WORKS

Matt was totally blindsided when his wife filed for divorce, although he'd been seeing the warning signs for months. Instead of panicking, he spent sixty days quietly implementing the Four Pillars. He documented his parenting, organized his finances, and assembled his support team. When the divorce process started, he already had. Result: equal custody, fair financial settlement, and a smooth process that took eight months instead of being dragged over the coals for two years.

Marcus faced a high-conflict divorce with a wife who made false allegations and tried to weaponize their kids. But Marcus had prepared. He had recordings of conversations, detailed parenting journals, and character witnesses primed and ready to testify. The false allegations were exposed because he could prove what actually happened. Result: primary custody of his children *and* protection from financial manipulation.

David used his divorce experience to build a successful business helping other men. Rather than letting the process shatter his finances, David educated himself, chose collaborative approaches where possible, and maintained focus on his relationship with his daughter throughout. Result: financial stability, strong co-parenting relationship, and a firm foundation for future success.

These men succeeded because they approached divorce strategically rather than emotionally. Easier said than done? Yes, but the key is that they prepared for what was coming instead of just reacting to what was happening.

HOW THIS BOOK WILL TRANSFORM YOUR SITUATION

This book is organized along the divorce timeline — from recognizing the warning signs to building your new life afterward — and divided into five parts that do the following:

Part One: The Wake-Up Call helps you recognize when divorce is coming and why most men get caught off guard.

Part Two: The Preparation Phase teaches you the Four Pillars Framework and how to build your professional team.

Part Three: The Battle Phase runs you through the active divorce process, from avoiding early mistakes to winning custody and protecting assets.

Part Four: The Resolution Phase demonstrates how to negotiate agreements that actually protect your interests long-term.

Part Five: The Phoenix Phase guides you through navigating the first year after divorce, building the foundation for the very best rest of your life.

Each chapter includes real stories, practical tools, and specific action steps. You'll also get conversation scripts, financial calculations, documentation strategies, and assessment tools to apply these concepts to your unique situation.

SHIELD YOURSELF: THE REALITY CHECK

Before going further, take this honest assessment of your current situation:

Is your marriage thriving, surviving, or dying? Consider how your wife treats you compared to six months ago.

How much time does your wife spend on her phone, computer, or away from home without clear explanations?

Secret communications and vague explanations of plans can be signals of emotional affairs.

Are you walking on eggshells, avoiding topics that used to be normal conversations? This suggests your wife has already mentally checked out.

Does your wife avoid physical contact, show irritation at your presence, or seem happiest when you're not around? These behaviors indicate the marriage is already over in her mind.

Have friends or family members made comments about your marriage or your wife's behavior? Outside observers often see problems before we do.

If you answered yes to several of these questions, divorce may be closer than you think. But you're **NOT** powerless. You just need to start thinking strategically about protecting your interests and your children's wellbeing.

ONE MOVE THAT MATTERS

This week, start a private journal documenting your daily interactions with your children—activities you do together, conversations you have, and ways you contribute to their lives. Developing this simple habit now will lay the foundation for equal custody later.

Don't wait until divorce papers are filed. Start building your case for being a great father today.

YOUR STRATEGIC CHOICE

You have two options:

1. Hope everything works out, and wing it if your marriage ends
2. Prepare strategically to systematically protect yourself, regardless of what happens.

Careful planning doesn't mean giving up on your marriage.

It means being responsible for your family's future, regardless of how things turn out.

You're about to read real men's stories, although their names have been changed to protect their identities. Men who faced the same choice you're facing now. Men who prepared strategically — protecting their children, their finances, and their futures — and men who didn't prepare, who paid a much higher price.

Don't get screwed. Choose wisely.

―――――

Key Takeaways: Divorce outcomes are determined by careful planning, not luck or fairness. The Four Pillars Framework — protecting your money, children, freedom, and sanity — lays the foundation for navigating divorce successfully. Men who prepare strategically don't just survive divorce; they emerge stronger and build better lives for themselves and their children.

―――――

EMERGENCY QUICK-START GUIDE

IN CRISIS? READ THIS FIRST

Maybe she just said, *"I want a divorce."*

Maybe you were just served papers.

Maybe you have a meeting with a lawyer tomorrow and you're panicking.

Stop. Breathe.

This is survivable — but only if you act strategically.

Here's what you need to do **right now**, before you turn another page.

48-HOUR SURVIVAL PLAN

1. Don't Move Out
Unless you're in physical danger, do *not* vacate the house. Moving out hands her leverage on custody, finances, and property.

2. Secure Key Documents
Grab and copy:

- Tax returns (last 3 years)
- Pay stubs (last 3 months)
- Bank, retirement, and credit card statements
- Mortgage/lease paperwork
- Insurance policies
- Kids' school and medical records

Put copies somewhere safe (cloud folder or with a trusted friend).

3. Open a New Email Account
Private, secure, not shared with your spouse. Use it for communicating with your lawyer, financial accounts, and all divorce communication.

4. Change Your Passwords
All of them... email, bank accounts, phone, cloud backups, social media. Use unique, strong passwords.

5. Start a Custody Journal
Write down:

- Every exchange with your kids
- Who takes them to school, practices, doctors
- Overnights and weekends

Be meticulous. This journal may become evidence.

6. Don't Send Emotional Texts
No rants. No promises. No admissions of guilt. Assume every word you type will become Exhibit A in court.

7. Take a Money Snapshot
List:

- Every account you have (checking, savings, retirement, investment)
- Debts (credit cards, loans)
- Monthly bills and income

Getting a clear picture of your money now will protect it later.

8. Schedule Consultations
Even if you think you'll settle peacefully, meet at least one experienced divorce attorney. Knowledge = leverage.

9. Protect Your Mental Health
This is a brutal process. Don't try to white-knuckle it alone. Call a trusted friend, find a therapist, and/or join a support group.

10. Commit to Strategy, Not Reaction
Every panic move now becomes a weapon against you later. From this moment forward, you play chess, not checkers.

WHAT TO DO BEFORE YOUR FIRST ATTORNEY MEETING

Bring these items to save time and money:

- Last 3 years of tax returns
- 3 recent pay stubs
- Bank/retirement account statements
- Credit card statements
- Mortgage/lease documents
- Insurance policies
- Custody journal (if started)

Walking into that meeting with this folder makes you look prepared, not desperate.

ONE MOVE THAT MATTERS

Don't let fear make your first move for you.

Just take one of these steps today — even if it's only opening a new email account or starting your custody journal. Small moves now compound into big advantages later.

PART ONE
THE WAKE-UP CALL

CHAPTER 1
WHEN GOOD MEN GET BLINDSIDED

Robert sat in his attorney's office, staring at papers he never thought he'd see. After twenty-two years of marriage, three kids, what he thought was a strong relationship had nosedived when his wife filed for divorce while he was on a business trip. The worst part? Not the surprise. It was realizing that she'd been planning this for months, all while he was completely unaware.

"I never saw it coming," Robert told me. "Looking back, all the signs were there… I just didn't know what I was looking at."

You need to hear these stories. Not because I want to frighten you, but because recognizing how good men face serious setbacks is the first step to protecting yourself. These aren't stories about deadbeat dads or abusive husbands. They're guys who went to work every day, coached their kids' teams, and believed love would be enough to protect their families.

They were wrong.

The men you're about to meet made critical mistakes that cost them hundreds of thousands of dollars, years of limited time with their children, and devastated their financial futures. Every single mistake was preventable with the right knowledge and strategic action.

GEORGE'S STORY: THE AFFAIR HE IGNORED FOR SIX MONTHS

A hardworking electrician who married his high school sweetheart twenty-three years ago and had three children — Emma (16), Tyler (14), and Sophie (10) — George thought his marriage was solid, built on decades of shared history and mutual respect.

One crisp October day, he came home early feeling sick. As he approached the house, he recognized another parent's car in the driveway - someone from their kids' social circle. Not unusual, he thought, except all the children were at school and there was no reason for a midday visit.

George pulled up and sat there, confused. Something felt wrong. The blinds were drawn, which was strange in the middle of the day. And the house was too quiet. As soon as he opened the door, he knew. The guilty scrambling upstairs. The hushed voices. The sound of someone running across the bedroom floor above his head. George's wife was having an affair with their neighbor. In their bedroom. In the middle of the day.

What happened next was George's first critical mistake. Instead of documenting what he found or thinking strategically, George let his emotions seize the wheel. He confronted them immediately. He yelled. He threatened. Then he stormed out in a rage, with no plan and no evidence.

For six months, George tried to save his marriage. He attended counseling, begged, and promised to change. He ignored every red flag, convincing himself that love would fix what was broken. Meanwhile, his wife used those six months to prepare. She transferred money into accounts he didn't know about, consulted attorneys, and documented every argument. She portrayed herself as the victim of a hot-tempered husband, all while secretly planning her exit.

When divorce papers were finally filed, George discovered he had been completely outmaneuvered. His wife's attorney painted him as an unstable, angry man who had threatened his wife. The affair became secondary to his "threatening behavior." And those six months he spent diligently trying to save the marriage? They were six months of giving his wife a strategic advantage.

George lost his house, paid substantial alimony for nine years, and only got to see his children every other weekend. The total cost of his emotional reaction, instead of calculated decisions dictating his actions, was over $340,000, and a damaged relationship with his kids. George's mistake was choosing hope over strategy. When you discover evidence of betrayal, your first move should be documentation, not confrontation.

MATT'S STORY: THE SOCIAL MEDIA TRAP

Matt was a successful sales manager with a twelve-year marriage and two children: Jake (11) and Mia (8). Matt worked hard to provide for his family and enjoyed sharing their successes on social media — posting photos from business trips, golf outings with clients, and work achievements — all the while thinking he was showing the world how well he was doing.

What Matt didn't realize was that his wife, Sara, was carefully curating her own social media story. While Matt posted pictures of himself at conferences and client dinners, Sara posted pictures of herself at every school event, every soccer game, every dance recital. When Matt was traveling, Sara made sure to document herself handling bedtime routines, homework help, and sick days.

The narrative she wove became clearer over time. It made Matt out to be an absent father who prioritized work over family and her a dedicated mother, holding everything together while her husband focused on his career.

The breaking point came during Jake's championship baseball game. Matt was thrilled to attend. He was also stuck in traffic from a client meeting and so only arrived during the seventh inning, just as Jake hit the game-winning double. Matt was overjoyed to catch the most important moment, but Sara's social media post told a different story: "So proud of Jake for his amazing hit! Wish Dad could have been here to see it."

She never mentioned that Matt had coached the team all season, attended every practice, and helped Jake work on his swing for months. The post just showed a mother supporting her child, and a father being absent at the crucial moment.

When Sara filed for divorce six months later, she had three years of social media evidence to back up this alternate narrative of Matt as an absent father. Her attorney used these posts to argue for primary custody and higher support. They painted a picture of a mother who had been essentially single-parenting while her husband traveled for work.

Matt had no idea this evidence existed until that fateful day in a conference room when his own social media was used against him. The golf photos, work trips, and client dinners all looked damaging without context.

Matt's mistake was not understanding that everything he posted online could become evidence. In divorce, there's no such thing as harmless social media. Every post tells a story, and you need to make sure it's the right story.

JOSH'S STORY: COMING OUT DURING DIVORCE

Josh had been married for twelve years to a woman with whom he had two sons, David (10) and Ryan (8), before finally coming to terms with his sexuality. He was gay. Ending his marriage was the only way he could live authentically. In accordance with that sentiment, he approached the situation with what he believed was integrity and honesty. Josh told his wife the truth about his sexuality, suggested they handle divorce amicably through mediation, and offered to be fair about custody and finances.

He genuinely wanted to minimize damage to their children and maintain a civil relationship. What Josh didn't understand was that his wife felt devastated, angry, and betrayed by what she saw as years of deception. While he focused on being fair and honest, she focused on protecting herself and their children from what felt like an enormous betrayal.

The divorce Josh thought would take months through mediation festered into a bitter, three-year legal battle. His wife argued his "deception" made him an unfit parent and claimed he had exposed the family to health risks. She locked horns with every aspect of the settlement, turning each negotiation into an emotional battlefield.

Josh's commendable desire to be authentic clashed with the cold legal reality of divorce. His sexuality was weaponized in court. His attempts at fairness were seen as admissions of guilt. His honesty about his past struggles was twisted into evidence of instability.

By the time the smoke cleared, Josh had spent over $80,000 in legal fees to finalize their divorce, lost significant custody time with David and Ryan, and paid far more in support than originally discussed. His attempt to do the right thing without strategic planning nearly cost him his relationship with his children.

Josh's mistake was confusing honesty and being true to himself with strategy. Putting your hands up isn't the same as handing your spouse ammunition to use against you in court.

ROGER'S STORY: THE YOUNG PROFESSIONAL'S TWO-YEAR CUSTODY BATTLE

Roger was twenty-six when his marriage fell apart. They'd been together since middle school, through college, and into their first years of adult life. Their son, Connor, was only six months old when divorce proceedings began.

Roger thought his case would be straightforward. He was employed in sales, had no history of problems, and wanted to remain an active father. What he didn't anticipate was how the family court system would view a young father of an infant.

Despite Roger's desire to be involved, the initial custody arrangement gave him minimal time. The logic seemed simple: baby Connor needed his mother, especially for nursing, and Roger worked full-time while his wife stayed home. Every so-called 'temporary' arrangement solidified before his eyes, each becoming harder than the last to change, as the case dragged on.

Roger spent two years fighting for meaningful custody time with Connor. He attended every court hearing, followed every parenting plan to the letter, and documented his involvement carefully. The legal fees consumed his savings, forcing him into debt.

But that wasn't the hardest part - it was that his relationship with Connor during those tender, fleeting years developed only in snippets, through supervised visits and brief exchanges. Roger missed his son's first words, first steps, and countless other everyday moments that build father-child bonds.

By the time their divorce was finalized, Roger had achieved a fairer custody arrangement. But it came at an enormous cost. Two years of limited access during Connor's earliest phases of development couldn't be recovered. You can't put a price on these things. The same isn't true of failing to understand how temporary arrangements often become permanent: $65,000 in legal fees.

Roger's mistake was not understanding that fathers must fight strategically, and from day one. Initial temporary arrangements often become anchors which permanent custody decisions are tied to.

ADAM'S STORY: WHEN YOUR SPOUSE HAS PERSONALITY ISSUES

Adam wasn't just dealing with a spouse who wanted out - he was dealing with a spouse who wanted to destroy him. She'd always been difficult. Mood swings. Explosive anger over minor issues. An inability to take responsibility for problems. But Adam had learned to manage it, to walk on eggshells, to keep the peace for the sake of their two daughters, Sophia (12) and Isabella (9).

When Adam finally suggested they needed counseling, his wife's response was to file for divorce and immediately claim he was abusive. She filed a restraining order after an argument in which he raised his voice. She told Sophia and Isabella "Daddy is dangerous." She posted on social media about being a "survivor." Adam had never laid a hand on his wife or children. He'd never even cursed at her. But in the world of family court, accusations carry weight... even without evidence.

That restraining order meant Adam couldn't see his daughters or enter his own home. He had to find temporary housing, hire attorneys, and vigorously defend his innocence. All the while, every interaction between them became potential evidence against him. Every text message was scrutinized for signs of "harassment."

Adam's wife weaponized the court system. When he tried to exercise court-ordered visitation, she claimed the children were "afraid." When he sent birthday gifts, she said he was "violating boundaries." When he attended school events, she called it "stalking."

After three years and over $150,000, Adam eventually gained meaningful custody time, but the fracturing of his relationship with his daughters was severe. Having spent crucial years hearing that their father was dangerous, rebuilding their trust took years of patience and consistency.

Adam's mistake was not recognizing the signs of a high-conflict personality disorder and not preparing for the systematic campaign that followed. When you're married to someone who operates this way, normal divorce strategies simply don't work.

THE PATTERN BEHIND EVERY STORY

Those five men made different mistakes, screwing themselves in these ways:

1. **Reacting emotionally, not thinking strategically.** They let emotions drive their early decisions instead of considering long-term consequences.
2. **Failing to document important evidence.** George didn't document the affair, Matt didn't consider how his social media looked, Roger didn't build a case for his parenting involvement early enough.
3. **Underestimating their spouse's preparation.** All five assumed their wives would be fair, or at least reasonable, not understanding that divorce often brings out behaviors they'd never seen before.

4. **Trusting the system to be fair.** They believed that judges would see the truth, that good intentions would be rewarded, and that the system would protect children's best interests automatically.
5. **Giving their spouses time to prepare, while doing nothing themselves.** Each man spent months, or years, hoping things would improve while their wives were getting ready for battle.

THE GOOD NEWS: EVERY MISTAKE IS PREVENTABLE

Believe it or not, there's something encouraging about these stories: every single mistake these men made can be avoided with the right knowledge and calculated decisions.

George could have documented the affair and consulted an attorney before confronting anyone.

Matt could have been more careful about his social media presence and built his own documentation of involved parenting.

Josh could have prepared strategically before revealing his situation.

Roger could have fought for meaningful custody from day one, instead of accepting temporary arrangements.

Adam could have recognized the warning signs and prepared for a high-conflict divorce.

This is worth repeating:
The difference between men who get screwed and those who nail their divorce isn't intelligence, income, or luck. It's understanding the rules of the game and playing strategically rather than emotionally.

Shield Yourself: The Early Warning Assessment

Honestly assess your current situation with these criteria:

Relationship Stability: If someone objective looked at your marriage right now, would they say it's thriving, surviving, or struggling? Think about your wife's behavior toward you - has it changed in recent months?

Communication Patterns: Are you fighting more and connecting less? Has she mentioned being "unhappy" or suggested counseling? Has she become more critical or distant?

Financial Changes: Have you noticed new accounts, secretive spending, or unusual interest in your assets? Has she asked detailed questions about your income or benefits?

Social Media Story: What story does your combined social media presence tell about your marriage and your role as a husband and father? Would a divorce attorney see you as an involved father and devoted husband?

Children's Relationship: Are you consistently involved in your children's daily activities, school events, and important moments? Can you document this involvement?

If your honest answers reveal warning signs, it's time to stop hoping and start preparing strategically.

ONE MOVE THAT MATTERS

This week, conduct a simple social media audit. Look at the last six months of your posts and your wife's posts. What story do they tell about your marriage and your role as a husband and father? If a divorce attorney were building a case about your family, what kind of narrative would these posts support?

Start thinking about every digital footprint as potential evidence. Sound paranoid? It's not. It's strategic awareness. Begin documenting your involvement with your children through photos, calendar entries, and active participation in their activities.

The men who navigate divorce successfully understand that preparation today prevents problems tomorrow.

YOUR CHOICE STARTS NOW

You have a choice to make. You could hope things work out and wing it if they don't — like George, Matt, Josh, Roger, and Adam did — or can prepare strategically to protect yourself, regardless of what happens.

Expensive lessons were learned by those five men about the reality of divorce in America. Your education doesn't have to come at such a high cost.

While tough to admit sometimes, careful planning requires acknowledging that your marriage might be in trouble, even (and especially) when you're not ready for that reality. It requires thinking systematically when you'd rather think emotionally. It requires accepting hard truths about how divorce actually works, not how you hope it works or how it should work,

Here's the encouraging news: every mistake they made was preventable. Every trap they fell into can be avoided, and every costly error sidestepped. It just takes the right mindset and methodical approach.

The system can be navigated successfully by those who understand the rules and approach the process strategically. You just need to learn from their expensive mistakes rather than make your own.

Key Takeaway: Good men hit serious divorce setbacks not because they're bad husbands or fathers, but because they fail to recognize warning signs and prepare strategically. Every challenging divorce outcome in this chapter was preventable with the right preparation and mindset. Nailing your divorce requires understanding the rules and approaching the process strategically, not emotionally.

CHAPTER 2
RECOGNIZING THE POINT OF NO RETURN

David thought his marriage was fine… until he found an attorney's business card in his wife's purse. She'd been planning to divorce him for eight months, all while he was planning their anniversary trip to Hawaii! That business card changed everything — not because she wanted a divorce, but because it showed him how unprepared he was for what was coming.

Most men aren't blindsided in divorce because the signs weren't there, but because they didn't know how to read them. Women typically spend months, even years, mentally preparing before they ever say the words "I want a divorce." By the time that conversation happens, they've often consulted friends, researched attorneys, opened separate accounts, and emotionally detached from the marriage.

Understanding this process can be the difference between scrambling to catch up and being thoroughly prepared for whatever happens next.

HOW MEN AND WOMEN PROCESS MARRIAGE PROBLEMS DIFFERENTLY

So many good men getting caught off guard all comes down to the differences between how men and women approach relationship problems. Men tend to focus on solving immediate issues as they arise. Problem? We want to fix it. We want to move forward. Women often think more holistically, considering whether the relationship is making them happy overall.

This opens up a dangerous gap. While you're focused on handling individual problems, she may be asking herself bigger questions: "Am I fulfilled in this marriage? Do I want to spend the next twenty years feeling this way? What would my life look like if I were single again?"

By the time she's decided she wants out, she's likely already worked through the fear, guilt, and logistics. She's mentally ready for the change. Meanwhile, you've been faithfully trudging along, operating under the assumption that you're both working toward the same goal of staying married.

Take Roger from Chapter 1. He thought they were having normal arguments about his work schedule. She was documenting those arguments to build a case that he was an absent father. Same conversations, completely different spin.

THE CRITICAL WARNING SIGNS YOU CANNOT IGNORE

Forget subtle hints or normal marriage challenges; these are flaming red flags that signal potential divorce. If you recognize multiple signs from this list, it's time to start paying serious attention.

She's Building a Social Media Case

Sarah had barely posted about her family in two years. Suddenly, she's sharing photos of herself with the kids at every school event, posting about family dinners, and writing heartfelt captions about being a devoted mom. Wow, her husband thought, how sweet. It seemed positive to him... until his attorney explained what was really happening.

Sarah wasn't celebrating their family life — she was amassing evidence. She was building a narrative for future custody discussions that would depict her as the engaged, present parent. The timing wasn't coincidental. It started the same month she first googled "how to file for divorce in New Jersey." Watch for sudden increases in family-focused social media posts, especially if your wife historically hasn't been very active online. This is often preparation, not celebration.

Financial Behavior Changes Without Explanation

Money tells the real story. When someone starts preparing for divorce, they often begin restructuring their finances. This might look like opening a separate savings account "for household expenses," suddenly taking a deeper interest in the family's financial documents, or making purchases without the usual discussion beforehand.

Huh, Tom thought, when he noticed his wife had opened a new credit card. No big deal, I guess. That is, until he found out during divorce proceedings that she'd been using it to pay an attorney for three months. The separate card meant no statements would come to the house and no charges would show up on their shared accounts.

Other financial warning signs include taking over bill-paying responsibilities if she hasn't before, asking detailed questions about your retirement accounts, or changing direct deposit arrangements. Such actions often reflect someone preparing to fully separate their financial life from yours.

She Stops Being Your Person

Undeniably, one of the best parts of marriage is having someone there to listen when you need to talk. Whether celebrating good news or venting about a bad day, your spouse is supposed to be your go-to person. When that stops, the strong emotional connection likely does too.

If your wife stops sharing her day with you, stops asking about yours, or seems disinterested when you want to talk, she may be emotionally pulling away. This is especially worrying if she's begun confiding in friends or family members about things she used to discuss only with you.

Language shifts are important too. Notice when she switches from "we" to "I" as she talks about the future. Instead of saying "we should plan a vacation next summer," she says "I'm thinking about taking the kids somewhere next summer." This kind of linguistic change often shows a mental shift — she's already starting to see her life separately from yours in her mind.

Behavioral Changes That Feel Out of Character

When someone you've lived with for years suddenly feels like a different person, there's usually a reason. Perhaps she's being more secretive with her phone, changing her routine without explanation, or developing new interests that don't include you.

The phone changes are particularly telling. If someone who used to leave their phone around starts taking it to the bathroom, keeping it face-down during dinner, or getting protective about text messages, they're likely having conversations they don't want you to see.

Conversations About "What If" Scenarios

Be alert to hypothetical discussions about divorce, separation, or what life would look like if you weren't together. These aren't idle curiosity — they're mental rehearsals. She's testing how these ideas sound out loud. She's gauging your reaction.

Other concerning conversation patterns include talking about friends who got divorced, especially emphasizing how much better their lives are now, mentioning the high costs of divorce, or asking questions about custody arrangements that seem academic but feel pointed. For example, if she discusses someone's parenting schedule and asks for your opinion or whether you think it's fair, make a note of it!

WHEN FAITH AND MARRIAGE COLLIDE

Sam grew up Mormon. His faith shaped everything about how he approached marriage and family. "In our faith, marriage isn't just a lifetime commitment — it's an eternal commitment," Sam explained. "When that gets severed, it really takes a huge toll on you spiritually."

Many men from devout religious or different cultural backgrounds face unique challenges when recognizing that their marriage is on the rocks. Your faith community may pressure you to keep trying, regardless of the circumstances. Well-meaning religious leaders might counsel reconciliation, even when your wife has already emotionally or physically left the marriage.

The "Stay Together for the Kids" Religious Pressure

Religious teachings about the permanence of marriage can fuel enormous guilt about even considering divorce, despite the fact that staying together is harmful to everyone involved. You may hear that divorce is always wrong, that you should endure any hardship for your family, or that your faith requires you to keep trying indefinitely.

But staying in a toxic marriage doesn't serve your children, your spouse, or yourself. Children aren't insulated. They're sponges who learn relationship patterns from watching their parents. Showing them what staying in an unhealthy relationship looks like can be more damaging than modeling how to handle difficult situations with dignity and wisdom.

When Religious Reconciliation Efforts Have Been Exhausted

If you've tried marriage counseling with religious leaders, followed faith-based marriage programs, and made sincere efforts to repair your marriage according to your beliefs, you're not abandoning your faith by acknowledging reality. Most religious traditions ultimately recognize that some marriages cannot be saved, and that protecting the well-being of children and families may require difficult decisions.

The point of no return isn't abandoning your values — it's applying them to protect what matters most when other solutions have failed.

UNDERSTANDING THE POINT OF NO RETURN

To be clear, the point of no return isn't when she says she wants a divorce. It's when she stops fighting for the marriage. When she starts planning her exit.

Just like getting engaged in the first place, the mental shift takes place gradually and usually unfolds months, even years, before the actual conversation.

George's wife reached the point of no return when she started the affair and opened the separate bank account. Matt's wife reached it when she began building her social media case. Josh's wife reached it when she started consulting attorneys. Roger's wife reached it when she began documenting his work demands.

Each of these men could've recognized the signs if they'd known what to look for. Instead, they kept devotedly hoping things would improve while their wives were methodically preparing.

Understanding this timeline is crucial because it changes your entire approach. If your wife has reached the point of no return, then marriage counseling, romantic gestures, or promises to change are unlikely to work. You need a strategic response that protects your interests and your children's well-being.

THE COST OF DENIAL AND DELAY

When men see warning signs but choose to ignore them, hoping things will get better, they create several serious problems for themselves and their families.

1. **Denial gives your wife more preparation time while you do nothing.** Every day spent hoping things will improve is another day she's planning and positioning herself. This puts you on the back foot if divorce does happen.
2. **Ignored problems tend to fester.** Small issues that could've been addressed early can often mushroom into major conflicts that require court intervention. What started as disagreements about parenting time can turn into formal custody battles if left unaddressed.

3. **Denial often prolongs children's exposure to conflict.** Parents who refuse to acknowledge marital problems usually end up creating more tension and uncertainty for their kids. The sooner you address reality, the sooner you can create stability.
4. **Denial puts you in a reactive position.** Instead of making strategic decisions about your family's future, you end up simply responding to your wife's moves. Reactivity rarely leads to favorable outcomes.

YOUR THREE CHOICES WHEN YOU SEE THE SIGNS

When you start recognizing warning signs, you have three basic options:

One: Ignore Them… and Hope

This is what George, Matt, Josh, Roger, and Adam did. They picked up on the concerning changes but chose to believe things would get better on their own. In every case, they were wrong, leaving them completely unprepared for divorce.

Two: Try to Fix Everything Without Understanding the Real Problem

Floating the idea of marriage counseling, planning romantic gestures, or promising to change specific behaviors aren't wrong, they're just unlikely to work if your wife has already mentally checked out of the marriage.

Three: Accept Reality, Start Preparing Strategically

This doesn't mean giving up on your marriage immediately! It means protecting yourself and your children, regardless of what happens next. It means getting educated about your rights, organizing your financial documents, and making damn sure you're prepared for multiple possible outcomes.

Most men choose the first two options, devotedly claiming that's the "right" thing to do. But if your wife has reached the point of no return, only the third choice actually protects your family's future.

TAKING ACTION WHILE PROTECTING YOUR MARRIAGE

Careful planning doesn't require you to assume the worst about your wife or check out of your relationship. It does require you to be responsible for your family's well-being, regardless of what decisions others make.

Start by quietly educating yourself about divorce law in your state. Understand what factors courts consider when deciding on custody, support, and asset division. It'll help you make better decisions about your marriage, not just your potential divorce.

Begin organizing your financial documents and getting clear about your complete financial picture. This serves you well, whether you're trying to rebuild your marriage or protect yourself in divorce. Financial transparency and organization benefit any relationship.

Document concerning behaviors or conversations, not to use against your wife later, but to help yourself make informed decisions about your family's future. If troubling patterns continue, you'll have clear information to discuss with professionals.

Most importantly, take care of you. We're talking physical *and* mental health. Whether you're working to save your marriage or preparing for life after divorce, you need to be at your best for your children and yourself.

Shield Yourself: The Marriage Reality Assessment

This exercise requires brutal honesty. Don't answer based on how you hope things are, or how they used to be. Consider only what's actually happening right now.

Rate your marriage in these five areas on a scale of 1–10, where 10 means excellent and 1 means serious problems:

1. **Daily Communication**: Do you and your wife talk meaningfully about your lives, feelings, and plans for the future?
2. **Physical and Emotional Intimacy**: Are you connecting regularly, both emotionally and physically?
3. **Shared Goals and Dreams**: Are you working toward the same vision for your family's future?
4. **Conflict Resolution**: When you disagree, do you work together to find solutions?
5. **Mutual Respect and Appreciation**: Do you both express gratitude and respect for each other regularly?

Now count how many warning signs from this chapter apply to your current situation:

- Social media behavior changes
- Financial secrecy or changes
- Emotional distancing or detachment
- Behavioral changes that seem out of character
- "What if" conversations about divorce or separation
- Phone or communication secrecy
- Language shifts from "we" to "I"
- Spending more time with divorced friends
- Loss of physical and/or emotional intimacy
- Making future plans that don't include you that seem out of character

If you scored an average of 6 or below, or if you identified three or more warning signs, you need to start preparing for the possibility of divorce while also working on your marriage.

This isn't giving up — it's being realistic and responsible.

ONE MOVE THAT MATTERS

This week, think about your conversations with your wife. Has she said or done things that raise a red flag based upon what you learned in this chapter? Can you see behavior changes now that you know what to look for? If you have any reason to think your wife is thinking of divorce, or you are now thinking about it, it is time to start getting strategic and planning for the possibility of divorce.

Key Takeaway: The point of no return in marriage isn't filing for divorce — it's when they stop fighting for the relationship and start forming their exit strategy. Men who recognize warning signs early have time to prepare strategically instead of just reacting emotionally. This preparation doesn't mean you're giving up on your marriage; it means you're taking responsibility for your family's future, no matter what decisions others make.

PART TWO
THE PREPARATION PHASE

CHAPTER 3
THE FOUR PILLARS OF DIVORCE PREPARATION

Robert had been an engineer for twenty years when his wife dropped the divorce on him. His analytical mind immediately went to work: hire a lawyer, divide the assets fifty-fifty, work out custody, move on. Boom. Done. Right? Three months later, he was living in a studio apartment, seeing his kids every other weekend, and wondering where half his retirement savings had gone!

 "I treated divorce like a math problem," Robert told me later. "I thought if I just followed the legal steps, everything would work out fairly. I had no idea how much preparation mattered."

Robert's ill-fated, logical approach is all too common among men facing divorce. We tend to think logically about the process without understanding that divorce isn't just a legal transaction — it's a complete life restructuring that requires strategic planning across multiple areas.

The men who thrive during and after divorce understand something crucial: success isn't about having luck on your side, or a great lawyer. It's systematic preparation across four critical domains that will determine your outcome.

WHY MOST MEN FAIL AT DIVORCE PREPARATION

When marriages end, most men make one of two mistakes.

1) Doing nothing. They hope things will work out, assume fairness will prevail, and wait until their wife files to start thinking seriously about their future. These men get blindsided by how complex and challenging divorce can be.

2) Doing too much but focusing on the wrong things. Going into overdrive, they immediately hire an attorney and start fighting about who gets what, without addressing the fundamental issues that will determine their long-term success. Sure, they win some battles, but they lose the war.

Both approaches miss the fundamental and essential truth about divorce: outcomes are determined mainly by what is done before formal proceedings even begin, not in court or during negotiations. This is why successful divorce outcomes require what I call the Four Pillars approach. Think of these as the four pillars holding up your entire divorce strategy. If any of them is weak, the whole structure can collapse. If not, they'll stand firm, protecting you regardless of how challenging the process becomes.

THE FOUR PILLARS FRAMEWORK

Pillar 1: Protect Your Money

Establishing financial protection and strategic planning that ensures you emerge from divorce with adequate resources to rebuild your life.

Pillar 2: Protect Your Children

Creating custody documentation and ensuring active involvement that positions you for meaningful time with your kids.

Pillar 3: Protect Your Freedom

Avoiding false allegations and legal troubles that can derail everything you're working toward.

Pillar 4: Protect Your Sanity

Safeguarding mental and physical health allows you to make good decisions throughout the process.

These pillars work together. Protecting your sanity helps you make better financial decisions. Protecting your children gives you motivation to stay focused on long-term goals. Protecting your money gives you resources to protect everything else. Protecting your freedom keeps you in the game when legal problems might sideline others.

Let me walk you through each pillar to illustrate what its successful construction looks like.

PILLAR 1: PROTECTING YOUR MONEY

Money problems destroy more post-divorce lives than anything else. Men who don't understand the financial realities of divorce often find themselves financially starting from scratch in their forties or fifties. And let me tell you, it isn't pretty when they're suddenly unable to retire when they planned and left struggling to maintain their standard of living.

The goal isn't to hide money or cheat your wife out of what's fair. The goal is to understand how divorce affects finances and position yourself for the best possible outcome within the legal framework so you don't end up like Robert, a senior engineer, living in a studio apartment.

Understanding Your Complete Financial Picture

Most men think they know their family's finances, but there's nothing like divorce to reveal how much they don't. Start by downloading seven years of statements from every financial account you have access to. Not two years, not three years — seven years. For every single account.

Save these documents in a secure cloud storage service where you'll always have access… you know, that new one I told you to create that has a new and secure password! Organize them by account and by date. You never want to be left anxiously looking for documents, or be caught with your pants down when statements have mysteriously disappeared as divorce proceedings begin.

Pay special attention to checking account details. Download images of checks (front and back) because most banks no longer include check copies with statements. You need to see who checks were written to, as well as who deposited them. These details often become important during financial discovery.

Creating Your Post-Divorce Budget

Here's an uncomfortable truth: your standard of living will probably dwindle after divorce. The question is by how much. Men who budget strategically minimize this impact. Men who don't often find themselves in dire financial straits.

Calculate what your life will actually cost as a single man. Studio apartments aren't great for anyone — especially since you're planning on having your children stay overnight — so budget for a bigger place, as well as increased food expenses since you'll lose economies of scale, separate utilities and insurance, and higher transportation costs for custody exchanges and separate activities.

Don't forget the hidden costs of divorce, like legal fees, therapy costs, duplicate household items, and increased childcare expenses when kids are with you. These expenses add up quickly, catching unprepared men off guard.

Income Strategy During Preparation

If possible, avoid significant income fluctuations during the preparation and divorce period. Courts often use current income as a benchmark to calculate ongoing support obligations, so a big raise right before divorce can increase your support payments significantly. However, if you've been underpaid or underemployed, consider whether strategic career moves might improve your long-term financial position. Just understand that increased income during divorce proceedings will likely lead to higher support obligations in the future.

Asset Protection Basics

Understand the difference between marital and separate property in your state. Generally, marital property includes assets acquired during marriage, regardless of whose name is on the title. Separate property includes assets owned before marriage, inheritances, and gifts given explicitly to one spouse. However, remember always to keep separate property separate. Don't use marital funds to improve premarital assets, unless you understand the consequences. If you owned a house before marriage but used joint funds for renovations, your wife might have a claim to the increased property value that resulted. Avoid comingling premarital money with marital money (like depositing your paycheck in an otherwise exempt bank account).

Document all valuable assets with photos and current valuations. Use Kelly Blue Book for vehicles, Zillow or Realtor.com for real estate estimates, and professional appraisals for valuable collections or business assets. Create a comprehensive inventory of anything worth more than five hundred dollars.

PILLAR 2: PROTECTING YOUR CHILDREN

If you have children, this pillar is more important than everything else combined. Your relationship with your kids is irreplaceable, so custody outcomes often shape your happiness and theirs for decades to come. Here's what most fathers don't understand: *custody battles aren't won by being a good father.* They're won by proving you're a good father in ways that family court judges understand and value.

The Documentation Reality

Just like any court, family court operates on evidence, not emotions. Mothers often have a documentation advantage because women are more likely to keep baby books, take photos of family activities, and generally document children's lives. This creates a paper trail that can appear to be greater involvement to a judge.

Start documenting your parenting involvement *immediately*. Open your phone's calendar app and make simple notes about your daily interactions with your children. "Took kids to school. Helped with math homework. Read bedtime stories." *Simple, consistent, and effective.*

Document everything: school drop-offs and pickups, homework help, bedtime routines, doctor appointments, school events, extracurricular activities, and weekend family activities. The goal is to be able to demonstrate in court that you're an involved, engaged parent who contributes meaningfully to your children's daily lives.

Building Relationships with Your Children's "People"

Courts pay attention to which parent knows the details of the children's lives and has relationships with important people in their lives. Don't know your children's teachers, coaches, doctors, and activity leaders? Start establishing those connections now. Introduce yourself at the beginning of each school year. Attend parent-teacher conferences. Join school email lists. Volunteer for field trips or classroom activities. Be present at practices, not just games. Help out with team events. Build relationships with other parents. Join the Parent-Teach Organization (PTO). These connections can become valuable witnesses if custody is ever questioned. When a judge or custody evaluator asks teachers or school administrators about which parent is involved in school activities, you want your name to come up naturally and positively.

Adjusting Your Schedule for Maximum Impact

Working sixty-hour weeks but wanting fifty-fifty custody? Courts will consider your actual availability alongside your intentions. Adjust your schedule during the preparation period so that consistent patterns are in place by the time custody is reviewed. Can you work from home more often? Can you modify your hours for morning drop-offs or afternoon pickups? Can you cut back on travel commitments? These adjustments demonstrate to courts that you prioritize your children's needs and are capable of dedicating significant time to parenting.

Creating Evidence That Speaks to Judges

Holiday pictures are great but focus on taking photos that show you actively engaging with your children in everyday life. Good photos capture moments like reading together, helping with homework, cooking, or doing activities. Steer clear of posed photos that lack genuine interaction.

Keep records of your financial contributions to children's activities, medical care, and school expenses. Courts want to see that you're not just emotionally involved but financially invested in your children's well-being.

Save communications with schools, coaches, and medical providers that show your involvement in decision-making about your children's lives. These records demonstrate that you're already functioning as an active co-parentNone.

PILLAR 3: PROTECTING YOUR FREEDOM

False allegations can destroy men's lives faster than almost anything else in divorce proceedings. Oh, you've got a desperate or vindictive spouse making accusations of verbal abuse, physical violence, or substance use problems? Congratulations, suddenly you're defending yourself instead of working toward a fair resolution.

I'm not encouraging paranoia — just preparation for situations that happen more often than most men realize.

Understanding Recording Laws

Check your state's recording laws now. Really. Do it immediately.

Are you in a one-party consent state? If so, you can record conversations you're part of without telling or informing the consent of the other person.

Consider recording all significant conversations with your spouse about children, finances, or relationship issues. Use your phone's voice recorder app and save files with dates and descriptions. These recordings can help protect you when allegations arise. When she claims you threatened her, you'll have the actual conversation. When she says you agreed to something you didn't, you'll have proof of what was actually said.

Documentation Strategy for Protection

Document concerning behaviors carefully and objectively. If your spouse has anger issues, substance abuse problems, or makes threats, keep detailed records of incidents with dates, times, names of witnesses, and objective descriptions of what happened. Take photos of any property damage stemming from arguments/altercations. Save threatening text messages or emails. Keep a log of incidents that concern you, especially anything involving your children's safety or well-being. This isn't about attacking your wife — it's about protecting yourself and your children if serious problems develop.

The Witness Factor

Whenever possible during divorce proceedings, avoid being alone with your spouse. Have witnesses present for custody exchanges, important conversations, or any time you're in the family home together. Public places with security cameras should be the venue for child exchanges — think police stations, libraries, or busy shopping centers where interactions are naturally witnessed — to protect both of you from false allegations and keep exchanges focused on the children.

Emergency Planning

If your situation involves domestic violence concerns, substance abuse, or serious mental health issues, you need an emergency plan in place before it is needed. Know where you'll go ahead of time if you need to leave quickly. Keep important documents stored in the cloud. Finally, have cash, your passport, and important original documents in a bag packed with essentials.

A bug-out bag? Call it whatever you like, but it's really about protection, not paranoia. Men with emergency plans rarely need to use them, but those without them often wish they had when situations suddenly worsen.

PILLAR 4: PROTECTING YOUR SANITY

Your mental and physical health aren't luxuries during divorce preparation — they're essential. Men who ignore this crucial aspect make poor choices that can cost them dearly in every part of their lives. Since divorce is one of the most stressful life experiences anyone can face, your ability to think clearly, make sound decisions, and keep perspective depends entirely on taking care of your body and mind.

Physical Health as Your Foundation

When stressed, many men abandon healthy habits just when they need them most. They skip exercise, eat poorly, drink too much, and ignore medical problems. The resulting downward spiral pulls everything else down with it. Schedule a complete physical exam and address any health issues you've been avoiding. Start or maintain a consistent exercise routine. Even thirty minutes of walking daily makes a significant difference in your mental clarity and emotional stability. Eat regular, nutritious meals and get adequate sleep.

I know... I know... these basics seem obvious, but they're often the first things men let slide when life gets complicated. Your body is the foundation for everything else you're trying to accomplish. Treat it accordingly.

Mental Health Strategy

Consider working with a therapist who specializes in men's issues or divorce transition. This isn't a sign of weakness — it's careful planning. A good therapist helps you process emotions in healthy ways, empowering you to make better decisions and maintain perspective during challenging times. Avoid toxic influences during this period. Some friends and family members will want to fan your anger instead of helping you heal. They mean well, but that's not helpful. Limit time with people who make you feel worse about your situation or encourage destructive behavior.

Building Your Support Network

Connect with other men who have successfully navigated divorce. Join support groups or online communities where you can learn from others' experiences. Having mentors who've been through the process helps you avoid common mistakes and maintain hope for the future.

Absolutely, definitely don't try to handle everything alone! Men often think they should be able to manage major life challenges without help, but divorce is too complex and emotionally charged for most people to navigate successfully without support. Maybe you can, but why test that theory?

The Mind-Body Connection

Your physical and mental health are directly connected. When you take care of your body through exercise and proper nutrition, your mind works better. When you manage stress through healthy outlets, your body stays stronger.

Limit alcohol consumption during this period. Of course, it might provide temporary relief from stress, but that comes at the cost of impairing judgment and decision-making when you need to be at your sharpest. And any hint of substance abuse in custody proceedings is not something you want muddying the waters.

Practice stress management techniques that work for you. Meditation, prayer, hobbies, or time in nature... it doesn't really matter what, just as long as you find healthy ways to process emotions and maintain balance during an inherently (and temporarily) unbalanced time in your life.

CULTURAL PREPARATION STRATEGIES

Building Cultural Support Networks

Your preparation phase must include strategies for managing relationships with cultural and religious communities. In many traditional communities, divorce affects not just you and your immediate family but entire extended networks of relatives, friends, and religious community members.

Begin identifying which community members will genuinely support and who might add stress through judgment or pressure. Reach out early to religious leaders, family members, or community elders who understand complex life situations, can empathize with those experiencing them, and offer realistic guidance rather than simple answers.

Consider reaching out to others from your cultural background who have successfully navigated divorce while keeping their faith and community ties. These relationships offer both practical advice and hope that you can protect what matters most about your cultural identity and safeguard your family's well-being.

Preparing for Community Reactions

Develop strategies for handling inevitable questions, assumptions, and opinions from your cultural community. Practice brief, dignified responses that maintain your privacy while preserving important relationships. Remember - you can't control what people think, but you can control how you act throughout the process.

SHIELD YOURSELF: FOUR PILLARS ASSESSMENT

Rate your current preparedness in each pillar's area on a scale of 1–10, where 10 means fully prepared:

Pillar 1 - Financial Protection:

- Do you have seven years of financial statements organized and accessible?
- Have you created a realistic post-divorce budget?
- Do you understand your state's asset division laws?
- Have you documented all assets worth over $500, with their current valuations?

Pillar 2 - Children Protection:

- Are you documenting daily parenting activities?
- Do you have relationships with your children's teachers, coaches, and activity leaders?
- Have you adjusted your schedule to maximize availability for parenting?
- Are you creating evidence of your involvement through photos and records?

Pillar 3 - Freedom Protection:

- Do you know your state's recording laws?
- Are you documenting any concerning behaviors of your spouse?
- Do you have an emergency plan in case situations escalate?
- Are you avoiding being alone with your spouse during sensitive conversations?

Pillar 4 - Sanity Protection:

- Are you maintaining regular exercise and proper nutrition?
- Have you considered seeking professional mental health counseling?

- Do you have healthy friends and mentors you can talk to?
- Are you managing stress through positive outlets rather than destructive ones?

If you scored below 7 in any pillar, you should prioritize taking immediate attention within it. If you scored below 5 in multiple pillars, you need to create a systematic plan to address each area over the coming weeks.

ONE MOVE THAT MATTERS

This week, choose your weakest pillar from the assessment and take one concrete action to strengthen it.

Financial Protection your weakest? Start gathering your financial documents. Download the last year of statements from three of your most important accounts and organize them in a secure cloud folder.

Children Protection? Begin your parenting journal today. Document every interaction with your children for the next seven days and save those records.

Freedom Protection? Research your state's recording laws and download a voice recording app to your phone. Practice with it to make sure you're familiar with how to use it.

Sanity Protection? Schedule a physical exam and commit to thirty minutes of exercise three times this week.

Start with one pillar, but don't stop there. Each pillar supports the others, and your overall success depends on building stability across all four areas over time.

Key Takeaways: Successful divorce outcomes require systematic preparation to protect four critical areas of your life: finances, children, freedom, and sanity. These pillars work together to create a foundation that protects you regardless of how challenging the divorce process becomes. Men who strengthen all four pillars before divorce begins have significantly better outcomes than those who emotionally react to problems as they arise.

CHAPTER 4
BUILDING YOUR DIVORCE TEAM

It's just like hiring a contractor to fix the roof, Marcus thought, as he began the process of hiring a divorce attorney — find someone with good reviews and a reasonable price, then let them handle everything. Six months later, his attorney had focused solely on legal issues while Marcus struggled with depression, made terrible financial decisions, and nearly lost his relationship with his kids because no one was helping him navigate the emotional and practical challenges.

 "I realized I was trying to perform surgery on myself," Marcus told me afterward. "My lawyer knew the law, but I needed help with so much more than just legal strategy."

Marcus learned what successful men understand from the beginning: divorce opens up cracks in every area of your life — legal, financial, emotional, and practical. You need specialists for each area, working together toward your goals to keep things together.

His analogy of going through divorce alone being like trying to perform complex surgery on yourself was fitting. You might survive, but you'll do unnecessary damage that could have been avoided with the right team.

WHY FRIEND ADVICE FAILS

Before we talk about building your professional team, let's address why your buddy's divorce advice probably stinks. Your friend means well. He survived his divorce, and wants to help you avoid his mistakes. But every divorce is unique. Different states have different laws. Financial situations vary dramatically. Children's ages matter. Different personalities of spouses create different challenges. Different family dynamics affect strategy. What worked brilliantly for your friend might be catastrophic for your situation.

Even worse, most people's memories of their divorce get fuzzy over time. They remember the big outcomes but forget the details of how they got there. The strategy that seemed brilliant in hindsight might have been pure luck at the time. Your uncle, who "represented himself and saved thousands," might have also given up custody rights he didn't understand, or agreed to support payments that seem small now but will create financial challenges in retirement.

Take Steve, for example. His brother convinced him that "all you need is a tough lawyer who will fight for you." Steve took that advice... and ended up hiring an aggressive attorney, turning a cooperative situation into a costly two-year court battle. The legal fees depleted most of the assets they were fighting over, and the fallout strained Steve's relationship with his children in ways that took years to mend.

Meanwhile, Steve's neighbor went through a similar divorce but used mediation and a collaborative team approach. It cost a fraction of what Steve's did, preserved family relationships, and created a foundation for successful co-parenting. Same type of marriage, same basic issues, completely different approaches and outcomes.

The lesson - get emotional support from friends but get strategic guidance from professionals.

THE TEAM APPROACH WORKS

In 2013, the American Bar Association recognized divorce coaching as the fourth essential element of the divorce process. They understood that there was extreme burnout among family law professionals and overwhelming emotional turmoil for clients. The solution? A coordinated team approach, wherein each professional handles their area of expertise.

Think of it like assembling a medical team for complex surgery. Each professional has specific expertise that the others don't. Your attorney understands the law but might not be trained in financial planning. Your therapist knows how to help you process emotions but can't give legal advice. Your financial advisor can analyze settlement scenarios but isn't qualified to help you communicate better with your ex.

When these professionals work together, they create a support system that addresses every aspect of your divorce challenge.

YOUR CORE DIVORCE TEAM

Not everyone needs the same lineup, but most successful divorces involve a similar squad of several key professionals working in coordination.

The Attorney: Your Legal Quarterback

If this were a football team, your attorney would be the quarterback - solid, with good fundamentals, who really knows their craft. You don't want a dabbler. You wouldn't ask a general practitioner to perform brain surgery. The same principle applies to divorce attorneys. You want someone who specializes in family law and spends all their time on divorce cases.

What Your Attorney Actually Does

Your attorney reviews all your Four Pillars preparation and explains what the law states. They outline what you're entitled to, what your wife is entitled to, then describe what will happen with your children based on your state's custody laws and guide you through what the process will involve. They will then represent your interests in negotiations and court, if needed.

Your attorney is your legal strategist, not your therapist, financial planner, or life coach. Understanding this distinction helps you use their expertise efficiently and cost-effectively.

Questions to Ask Potential Attorneys

When interviewing attorneys, ask how many divorce cases they handle per year and what percentage of their practice is dedicated to family law. Find out their approach to high-conflict versus collaborative cases and how they typically communicate with clients throughout the process. Get clear information about their fees and billing practices. And do it upfront. Ask them to give you a realistic range of possible outcomes for your situation and to explain how they work with other professionals, such as financial advisors or therapists.

Red Flags

Avoid attorneys who promise unrealistic outcomes like "I'll get you sole custody" without knowing the details of your case, those who immediately suggest aggressive tactics, and anyone who can't explain their strategy clearly. Don't hire attorneys who don't return calls promptly, seem to encourage unnecessary conflict, or make decisions without consulting you. If an attorney seems more interested in creating drama than solving problems, they're going to be one. Keep looking.

The Therapist: Your Mental Health Strategist

You need someone to help you make better decisions, not just feel better. A good divorce therapist helps you separate the emotional side from the business side of divorce. This isn't about lying on a couch, rambling on endlessly about your childhood. This is about developing practical coping strategies that allow you to function effectively during one of the most stressful experiences of your life.

What a Good Divorce Therapist Does

A skilled divorce therapist helps you process emotions without letting them drive your decisions. They teach you communication strategies for dealing with your ex, especially around children's issues, and provide coping mechanisms for high-stress situations that help you be a better parent during the transition.

Most importantly, they offer perspective when you're too close to the situation to see clearly. Fired up and ready to shoot off that angry text message at midnight? A good therapist will have earned their money by not only teaching you why that's a terrible idea — you probably know that already — but by giving you better alternatives.

Finding the Right Therapist

Look for a therapist experienced in divorce and familiar with men's issues. They should understand your legal constraints and be able to work with your other team members when necessary. Focus on practical coping strategies rather than just emotional venting. While processing feelings is important, you need someone who helps you function better, not just feel validated.

The Financial Advisor: Your Economic Strategy Specialist

Many men don't realize how much they need financial guidance during divorce until it's too late. Seem like an unnecessary expense? Consider that a financial advisor who understands divorce can save you significant money and help you make better long-term decisions.

Even if you're financially savvy, divorce creates unique challenges that require specialized knowledge. You're going from one household to two, potentially dealing with alimony payments, dividing retirement accounts, and making decisions about assets while under emotional stress.

What a Good Divorce Financial Advisor Does

A skilled divorce financial advisor analyzes different settlement scenarios and shows you the long-term financial impact of each option. They help you understand the true cost of keeping certain assets versus taking others and can create realistic post-divorce budgets based on your new financial reality. They identify tax implications of different settlement options that you might not consider, help you plan for retirement after dividing assets, and show you how to rebuild wealth strategically after divorce.

Look for a CDFA (Certified Divorce Financial Analyst)

If possible, find a Certified Divorce Financial Analyst. They specialize in divorce-related financial issues and understand nuances that regular financial advisors might not. They know how to evaluate the long-term value of different assets and can model various settlement scenarios for you.

The Divorce Coach: Your Strategic Coordinator

A divorce coach fills the gaps between your other professionals. Think of your divorce coach as your project manager — someone who helps coordinate all the moving parts and keeps you focused on your big-picture goals.

What a Good Divorce Coach Does

They can assist you in setting realistic priorities, allowing you to dedicate your time and energy to what truly matters instead of getting caught up in the details. They provide accountability for completing the preparation work that influences your outcome. They help you communicate effectively with other team members and teach negotiation strategies tailored to your specific situation. Additionally, they assist you in preparing for important meetings, mediations, and court appearances.

Most importantly, they provide emotional support with a strategic focus. While your therapist helps you process emotions, your divorce coach helps you channel those emotions into productive action.

THE SUPPORTING CAST

Depending on your specific situation, you might also need additional specialists in your corner:

Insurance Agent

Life insurance becomes crucial when you have children and potential alimony obligations. Health insurance coverage changes when you separate. Auto insurance policies often don't cover vehicles in different residences. An insurance professional who understands divorce can help you navigate these changes and avoid risky coverage gaps.

Real Estate Professional

If you own property, you need someone who understands the divorce implications of selling versus keeping real estate. Some agents specialize in helping divorcing couples and understand the emotional and financial complexities involved.

Mortgage Broker

Maybe you'll need to refinance to remove your ex from the mortgage or to qualify for a new mortgage on your own. Some brokers specialize in helping divorcing people handle these changing financial situations.

Forensic Accountant

If there are hidden assets, complex business valuations, or sophisticated financial arrangements, a forensic accountant can uncover what you need to know and present it in a way courts understand.

Child Psychologist

If you have children, a child psychologist can help them process the divorce and provide professional opinions about their needs and well-being that courts value highly.

Business Valuator

If you own a business, even a small LLC, you'll need a professional valuation to determine its worth for asset division purposes.

FINDING CULTURALLY COMPETENT PROFESSIONALS

Religious and Cultural Considerations

When building your divorce team, consider professionals who understand your cultural and religious background. This doesn't necessarily mean finding people who share it, but rather professionals who respect your values and understand how cultural factors impact divorce decisions.

David, a devout Catholic from a traditional Mexican-American family, faced enormous family pressure to reconcile despite his wife's ongoing addiction issues. His solution? Finding a Catholic counselor who understood both his religious obligations and the incompatible reality of his situation. With professional guidance, he was able to separate his family's cultural expectations from his religious obligations and make decisions that protected his children while honoring his faith.

Questions for Potential Team Members:

- How do you work with clients from traditional religious backgrounds?
- Have you handled divorces involving significant cultural or extended family pressures?
- Can you help me navigate my obligations to my faith community during this process?
- Do you understand the unique challenges of interfaith or intercultural marriages?

Working with Religious Leaders

If seeking guidance from religious leaders, choose those with real-life marital crisis experience rather than those who provide only theoretical or doctrinal answers. The most helpful religious counselors understand that protecting the well-being of children and families sometimes requires tough decisions that don't follow simple formulas.

HOW TO WORK EFFECTIVELY WITH YOUR TEAM

Set Clear Expectations

Each professional should understand what you're trying to achieve overall, what their specific role is in that, how you prefer to communicate, and how they should coordinate with your other team members.

Coordinate Communication

Don't let your team work in isolation. Your attorney and financial advisor should communicate about legal and financial trade-offs. Your therapist should understand the legal realities you're facing. Consider regular team meetings, even if only by phone, to ensure everyone is working toward the same goals.

Use Each Professional for Their Expertise

Don't ask your attorney for therapy or your therapist for legal advice! It sounds obvious, but people make this mistake. Use each professional for what they do best, and you'll get better results at a lower cost. As one professional told me, "You paid me to be qualified enough to talk about anything and smart enough to stop talking when I know I'm not qualified."

Be Completely Honest

Your professionals can only help if they know the truth, the full truth, and nothing but the truth. Hiding information, minimizing problems, or lying about finances will only hurt your case. Your team is bound by confidentiality and is on your side.

When to Fire Team Members

Sometimes you need to make changes to your team. There's nothing wrong with terminating any team member, including your attorney, if they're not serving your interests effectively.

Fire Your Attorney If

Consider changing attorneys if they don't return calls or emails within a reasonable time, can't explain their strategy or rationale for their advice, seem to make decisions without consulting you, encourage unnecessary fighting, or you've lost trust in their judgment.

Fire Your Therapist If

Change therapists if they're not helping you make better decisions, encourage you to make choices based purely on emotion, seem to take sides rather than help you process, or don't at least generally understand the legal constraints you're facing.

Fire Your Financial Advisor If

Consider changing financial advisors if they don't understand divorce-specific issues, can't explain long-term implications of their recommendations, try to sell you products rather than give advice, or can't work effectively with your other team members.

THE INVESTMENT MINDSET

Yes, building a professional team costs money. But think of it as an investment in your future rather than an expense. Good legal advice prevents costly mistakes that can affect you for years, costing much more in the long run. Similarly, good financial advice helps you make better long-term decisions about support and asset division. Good therapeutic support helps you make better decisions and be a better parent during a difficult transition. Good strategic coordination makes your other professionals more efficient and saves you money.

Mike learned this lesson the hard way. He tried to save money by handling his divorce with only a budget attorney who didn't specialize in family law and overlooked several key issues. Mike then made poor financial decisions out of stress, and his relationship with his children suffered because he lacked support to manage the emotional challenges. Mike's "cheap" divorce ended up costing him over $100,000 in mistakes that could have been avoided with proper professional guidance, which would have cost a fraction of that amount.

The cost of good advice is almost always less than the cost of poor outcomes.

SHIELD YOURSELF: TEAM ASSESSMENT STRATEGY

Evaluate what kind of professional help you need most right now based on your situation's complexity, your emotional state, your financial circumstances, and the level of conflict you're facing.

For Collaborative Situations with Straightforward Finances: Start with a family law attorney and a therapist. Add a financial advisor if you have significant assets to divide.

For High-Conflict Situations with Complex Assets: You'll need the full team from the beginning: attorney, therapist, financial advisor, and divorce coach. Consider additional specialists based on your specific issues.

For Uncertain Conflict Levels: Start with a divorce coach who can help you determine what other professionals you'll need as your situation develops.

Rate your current need for each professional:

- **Legal Guidance:** How simple are the legal issues you're facing?
- **Emotional Support:** How well are you managing the stress, and are you making good decisions that aren't clouded by emotion?
- **Financial Planning:** How comfortable are you with the financial implications of divorce?
- **Strategic Coordination:** How well are you managing all the moving parts of your divorce?

Any area where you things are complex or you are not doing well indicates you need professional help in that area.

ONE MOVE THAT MATTERS

This week, make three important phone calls that will either bring you peace of mind or prompt you to take action. Either outcome serves you well.

First, schedule a consultation with a family law attorney. Even if you don't hire them immediately, use this consultation to gain a deeper understanding of the legal landscape you're facing and your available options.

Second, book an appointment with a therapist who has experience with divorce and men's issues. Frame this as strategic support, not just emotional venting.

Third, arrange a meeting with a financial advisor who understands the implications of divorce. Bring your financial information from your Four Pillars preparation and ask them to help you understand what your post-divorce financial life might look like.

If you are more confused than ever about where to start, hire a divorce coach. They can help you figure out your next best step.

These conversations will help you understand the type of team you need and lay a foundation for the support system to carry you through this process successfully.

Key Takeaways: Professional guidance beats amateur advice every time. Building the right divorce team — attorney, therapist, financial advisor, divorce coach, and specialized professionals — is essential for navigating divorce successfully. Each professional serves a specific role, and coordination between them maximizes your outcome while minimizing costs. The investment in professional help almost always costs less than the consequences of poor decisions made without proper guidance.

PART THREE
THE BATTLE PHASE

CHAPTER 5
AVOIDING THE EARLY EXECUTION ERRORS

At 2:47 AM on a Tuesday night, David stared at his phone screen. Six hours of grueling arguing about custody schedules and support payments had led to this moment, when exhaustion finally won over strategy, as he typed fourteen words that would haunt him for years:

 "I don't care anymore. Take whatever you want. I just want this over with."

Those fourteen words cost David his retirement account, half his business, and — most importantly — his daily relationship with his children. One moment of emotional weakness. A lifetime of consequences.

The first 90 days of your divorce process are like the opening moves of a chess game. Make the right moves, and you set yourself up for success. Make the wrong moves, and you'll spend years trying to recover from decisions you made when you were hurt, angry, or just desperate to end the pain.

This is why early mistakes are so viciously devastating. You're not just making a bad decision for today — you're often making a decision that will affect you for the rest of your life.

WHY THE FIRST 90 DAYS DETERMINE EVERYTHING

Most men make their biggest mistakes in the first three months because they're operating from a place of emotion rather than strategy. The living arrangements you agree to "temporarily" often become permanent. The custody schedule you accept "just for now" and the financial arrangements you agree to "until we figure things out" become anchors that drag you down in all future negotiations.

Courts love stability and hate disruption. Any arrangement that seems to be working becomes the preferred arrangement in their eyes. What you intended as a short-term solution becomes your long-term reality. George from Chapter 1 learned this the hard way. He moved out of the house, thinking it would help things cool down while they worked things out, and that decision hurt his custody case for two years because courts saw his voluntary departure as evidence that he didn't consider the home essential to his relationship with his children.

Remember David? His angry late-night text message became evidence of his emotional instability and poor judgment. These weren't just momentary lapses — they were strategic disasters that cost them dearly.

The Moving Out Disaster

The biggest mistake I see men make is moving out of the family home too quickly. But look, I understand the impulse… the atmosphere is toxic, maybe there's been fighting, and you think giving everyone space will help. Or maybe your wife asks you to leave "for a while" until you figure things out.

Don't do it. Not without very careful consideration and not before seeking legal advice.

Why Moving Out Can Destroy Your Case

Moving out creates what courts call a "status quo" that they're hesitant to change. If you have children and you leave the house while they stay, you've just created evidence that the children are "stable" in their current situation with their mom as the main caregiver. Your temporary, well-meant decision becomes proof that changing the arrangement would be disruptive for the children.

The financial consequences of this compound quickly, since moving out doesn't eliminate your obligations to the house. You'll still be responsible for some or all of the mortgage, utilities, and maintenance, AND also be paying for your new living situation. This financial strain weakens your negotiating position and makes you appear financially irresponsible.

The person who stays in the house gains enormous advantages. They have physical control of important documents, children's belongings, and marital assets. They can change locks, control access to mail, and create barriers to your involvement in day-to-day family life. Courts also can view voluntary departure as evidence that you don't consider the house essential to your wellbeing or your relationship with your children. This perception undermines later claims that you need the house for custody purposes.

When You Might Need to Leave

Of course, there are legitimate reasons to move out, but they should be carefully considered and strategically executed. If there's genuine domestic violence, credible threats to your safety, or if staying creates an environment harmful to the children, temporary separation might be necessary. Still, if you must move out, do it strategically. Document the reasons for leaving in writing. Make it clear that the departure is temporary and establish a timeline for returning. Maintain all financial obligations to the house and establish a clear schedule for spending time with your children in the home.

Success Story: Staying Put Strategically

Robert's wife demanded he move out after she filed for divorce, claiming she needed "space to think." Robert consulted his attorney before packing his bags. They made a plan where Robert stayed in the house but moved to the guest bedroom, giving everyone space while keeping his legal position intact.

Robert continued his usual parenting duties, kept the house in order, and remained emotionally neutral during tense moments. The result? Robert kept equal custody and was awarded the house in the final settlement. "Moving out would have cost me everything," Robert told me later. "Staying put and staying civil saved my relationship with my kids and my financial future."

THE TEMPORARY AGREEMENT TRAP

Courts love temporary agreements because they provide structure during chaos. The problem is that, as we've covered, "temporary" often becomes permanent, especially if the arrangement appears to be working from the court's perspective.

Many men agree to temporary custody schedules, support payments, or living arrangements without understanding that by doing so, they are setting precedents that will be extremely difficult to change later. Their thinking is, "This is just until we figure things out," but the reality is that any arrangement lasting more than a few months becomes the new normal in the court's eyes.

Never Agree to Any Temporary Arrangement Without These Elements:

Every temporary agreement should have a set duration, typically no more than 90 days. After that period, the arrangement should either be renegotiated or reverted to its previous state. Don't accept open-ended "temporary" arrangements that could drift on indefinitely. Every temporary arrangement must be documented in writing, signed by both parties, and filed with the court if necessary. Verbal agreements are worthless in divorce proceedings and impossible to enforce when memories differ.

An agreement should also specify what circumstances would trigger a review or modification. This might include changes in income, living situations, or children's needs. Include automatic expiration dates that require both parties to actively renegotiate, rather than allowing unfavorable arrangements to become permanent by default.

Learning from Matt's Second Chance

Remember Matt from Chapter 1? During his second divorce, he applied lessons from his first disaster. When his second wife requested temporary support that seemed excessive, Matt insisted on a sixty-day written agreement with specific review triggers based on accurate financial information. The temporary arrangement expired as scheduled, forcing real negotiations based on facts rather than panic-driven assumptions. Matt saved thousands in support payments by refusing to let temporary become permanent.

COMMUNICATION LANDMINES

Your communications during divorce can serve as evidence. Every text message, email, voicemail, and social media post may be used to build a case about your character, fitness as a parent, financial status, and mental health. Most men don't understand this reality until it's too late. They send angry texts at 2 AM. They argue via email about child support. They post passive-aggressive messages on social media. They leave rambling voicemails, devotedly — and hopefully not drunkenly — trying to "work things out." All of this becomes evidence against them.

The Professional Communication Rules

Limit communication with your spouse to essential business matters pertaining to children, finances, or legal proceedings. No discussions about the relationship, your feelings, or attempts at reconciliation through text or email.

Use written communication instead of phone calls whenever possible. Written communications create records that protect you from false claims about what was said. But it works both ways. So, remember that everything you write can become a screenshot used in court. Write every message as if it will be read aloud to a judge, because it might be. Stay factual, professional, and emotionally neutral regardless of how your wife communicates with you.

Don't respond immediately to inflammatory messages. Wait at least one hour, ideally twenty-four hours, before responding to anything emotional or inflammatory. Most problems resolve themselves when you don't feed them with immediate reactions. Save all communications from your spouse. Screenshot text messages before they can be deleted. Save voicemails. Create backup copies of important email exchanges.

The co-parenting App Solution

Consider using specialized co-parenting communication apps like Our Family Wizard, TalkingParents, or AppClose. These platforms create verified records of all communications, offer scheduling for custody exchanges, and often include professional oversight options that courts respect. These apps also prevent informal texting that can lead men into communication traps. When you use a formal platform, you naturally communicate more professionally.

MANAGING CULTURAL STIGMA AND FAMILY PRESSURE

The Cultural Assumption Problem

In many traditional communities, automatic assumptions arose about who's "at fault" when a marriage ends. Sam experienced this firsthand: "Typically, the first thought is, 'Oh man, they're getting divorced, so what did he do? Have an affair? Beat her up?' That's something I confronted."

Such assumptions pile additional stress onto an already difficult, stinking heap of it. You're not just dealing with the end of your marriage — you're potentially dealing with damage to your reputation and standing in your community based on speculation rather than facts.

Strategies for Managing Community Relationships:

- Maintain your dignity and integrity regardless of what others assume or say
- Continue participating in your faith community if it provides strength, but be prepared for awkward situations
- Focus on people who judge you by your character and actions rather than your marital status
- Avoid defending yourself against every rumor or assumption — your conduct will speak volumes for itself

Extended Family Boundary Setting

Cultural backgrounds with strong extended family involvement can lead to situations where grandparents, aunts, uncles, and cousins feel entitled to voice their opinions about your marriage and divorce decisions. Set clear boundaries regarding which aspects of your divorce are open for family discussion and which remain private.

You can appreciate family concern while maintaining your right to make decisions based on your specific circumstances rather than their expectations. Practice responses like: "I appreciate your concern, but this is something [spouse] and I need to work through with our counselor/attorney."

Interfaith and Intercultural Considerations

If your marriage crossed cultural or religious boundaries, divorce can weave additional threads of complexity around your children's cultural identities and extended family relationships. Work to preserve your children's connection to both cultural backgrounds, while also acknowledging that some relationships may become more challenging to maintain.

THE SOCIAL MEDIA BLACKOUT

Tread carefully. Social media during divorce is a minefield. The happy vacation photos you post can be used to argue you're hiding income or have more income than you are reporting. That much-needed night out with friends becomes evidence of irresponsible behavior. The new relationship you thought was private becomes evidence of poor judgment or adultery.

The safest approach is complete social media silence during divorce proceedings. Don't post anything, don't comment on others' posts, and definitely don't engage with your spouse's social media in any way.

If You Must Maintain Social Media

If professional obligations require a social media presence, follow strict guidelines. Share only work-related content — avoid personal opinions, photos, or lifestyle details — and never share photos or information about your children during divorce proceedings. Secure all privacy settings and block or remove your spouse from all platforms.

Be very cautious when deleting previous posts. Courts might interpret deleting potentially unfavorable content as evidence destruction. If you need to clean up your social media history, do so through your attorney to prevent legal issues.

The Recording Reality

Assume every conversation with your spouse is being recorded. In many states, only one party needs to consent to recording, so your spouse may be legally recording you without telling you.

This means every word you say can become evidence. Never make threats, even joking ones. Don't admit to things you didn't do just to end an argument. Avoid discussing finances, relationships, or anything that could be taken out of context later.

If your state allows one-party consent recording, consider recording your own conversations for protection. These recordings can be invaluable when false allegations arise.

PROTECTING YOURSELF FROM FALSE ALLEGATIONS

False allegations can screw your divorce faster than almost anything else. Accusations of abuse, violence, or substance problems can result in restraining orders, loss of custody, and even criminal charges.

Proactive Protection Strategies

Whenever possible, avoid being alone with your spouse during divorce proceedings. Have witnesses present for custody exchanges, important conversations, or any time you're in the family home together.

Choose public places equipped with security cameras for child exchange meetings. Meet at police stations, libraries, or busy shopping centers where interactions are naturally observed and recorded.

Document any threats or false claims made by your spouse. Keep evidence of your normal, healthy behavior and parenting. Spouse have a history of making false claims or exhibiting unstable behavior? Document it carefully, including dates, times, and witnesses.

If false allegations are made, don't panic or retaliate. Contact your attorney immediately. Gather evidence that disproves those claims — text messages, witnesses, documentation of your activities. Follow all court orders, even temporary ones based on false claims, because fighting them the wrong way makes everything worse.

FINANCIAL MISTAKES THAT COMPOUND

The financial decisions you make in the first 90 days often determine your financial outcome for years to come. Many men make these decisions based on guilt, anger, or the desire to "just get it over with," which ends up costing them tens of thousands of dollars.

Don't voluntarily assume all the marital debt to "be nice" or out of guilt. Don't agree to support payments without knowing how they're calculated. Don't give up retirement accounts without understanding their true value compared to other assets.

Open a separate checking account for your income, but don't hide assets or try to shelter money inappropriately. Pull your credit reports and freeze your credit if necessary to prevent new debt from being created in your name.

Document all valuable assets with photos or video. Change passwords on all your personal accounts, but don't change passwords on joint accounts without legal guidance.

SHIELD YOURSELF: THE 90-DAY SURVIVAL CHECKLIST

Weeks 1–2: Immediate Protection

- Do NOT move out of the family home without legal advice
- Open a separate checking account for your income only
- Pull credit reports and freeze credit if necessary to prevent unauthorized accounts
- Document all valuable assets with photos/video
- Change passwords on personal accounts (not joint accounts)
- Start using co-parenting communication app for all spouse interactions

Weeks 3–4: Communication and Evidence

- Implement complete social media blackout
- Review and carefully consider deleting potentially problematic social media history
- Establish conversation recording routine, if legal in your state
- Create witness plan for future interactions with spouse
- Begin documenting any concerning behaviors of spouse, with dates and details

Month 2: Review and Adjust

- Review all temporary agreements for specific time limits and modification triggers
- Evaluate custody arrangements and document any problems or needed changes
- Assess financial arrangements and adjust if not serving your interests
- Continue strict professional communication practices

Month 3: Preparation for Next Phase

- Complete 90-day evaluation of all temporary arrangements
- Document any course corrections needed for ongoing proceedings
- Prepare comprehensive evidence package for next phase of divorce
- Ensure all protective measures are working effectively

WHEN COURSE CORRECTION IS NEEDED

Made mistakes in the first 90 days? Your situation isn't hopeless, but it requires calculated decisions and often professional help.

Fixing Custody Problems

If you've allowed a custody arrangement that doesn't serve your children's interests or your relationship with them, you'll need to build a compelling case for why change benefits the children. This requires documentation showing how the current arrangement isn't working, evidence of your increased involvement and capabilities, and often professional support from child therapists or custody evaluators.

Addressing Financial Mistakes

Financial mistakes in early divorce proceedings can often be corrected, but this requires clear documentation of why the current arrangement isn't working, professional analysis showing accurate calculations, and a willingness to stand firm in negotiations rather than accepting unfavorable terms out of guilt or exhaustion.

Communication Cleanup

If your communication has been less than ideal early on in the process, stop making the same mistakes immediately! Consider using structured communication tools and focus on professional, factual communication only going forward. Sometimes, a sincere apology for poor communication can actually help your case, but ensure it is handled properly through your attorney.

THE MARATHON MINDSET

The men who emerge from divorce successfully understand that divorce is a marathon, not a sprint. They avoid emotional reactions that feel good in the moment but create long-term consequences. They think systematically about every decision, understanding that temporary choices often become permanent realities.

The decisions you make in the first 90 days lay the foundation for everything that follows. Nail this phase, and you'll have momentum and a strong negotiating position. Get it wrong, and you'll spend the rest of your divorce trying to scramble out of holes you dug when you were emotional and unprepared.

ONE MOVE THAT MATTERS

This week, conduct a comprehensive audit of every "temporary" arrangement you've agreed to in your divorce. Ask yourself these critical questions for each one:

Does it have a specific end date? If not, it's not temporary — it's permanent until someone forces a change.

Is it documented in writing and signed by both parties? If not, you have no enforceable agreement.

Does it serve your long-term interests and increase children's well-being? If not, you need to address it before it becomes entrenched.

If the answer to any of these questions is no, contact your attorney immediately to discuss modifications, clarifications, or exit strategies.

Remember, early mistakes in divorce compound over time. The goal isn't perfection — it's leveraging calculated decisions that protect your future while maintaining your integrity throughout the process.

Key Takeaways: The first 90 days set the trajectory for your entire divorce. Avoid making emotional decisions that feel seductively satisfying in the moment but screw you in the long-term. Never agree to open-ended temporary arrangements. Assume all communications could become potential evidence. Protect yourself from false allegations through witnesses and documentation. Think systematically about every decision, understanding that temporary choices often become permanent realities in family court.

CHAPTER 6
THE MEDIATION VS. LITIGATION DECISION

THE $42,000 QUESTION

 "You can either put your kids through college or put your attorney's kids through college."

That's what Rick told me after spending $42,000 in legal fees on a case that settled on the courthouse steps... for exactly what his wife had offered in mediation eighteen months earlier. Rick's story shows us the most important truth about divorce strategy: **the battlefield you choose determines the war you fight.**

Rick kicked off his divorce by hiring the most aggressive attorney in town. He did that because he was angry at his wife for having an emotional affair with a coworker, and wanted to "make her pay." Eighteen months later, Rick had his victory — and his kids qualified for financial aid because he'd spent their college fund on lawyers!

 "I got caught up in being right instead of being smart," Rick admits today. "My attorney kept telling me we could get more if we fought harder. What he didn't tell me was that 'more' might not be worth what it would cost to get it."

Today, Rick has rebuilt his relationship with his kids and his finances. But he learned an expensive lesson: **your choice of resolution process often matters more than the specific details you're fighting about.**

UNDERSTANDING YOUR STRATEGIC OPTIONS

Right now, you're standing at the precipice of making the most important decision in your divorce. You've done your Four Pillars preparation. You've built your professional team. Now comes the choice that will determine your timeline, costs, stress level, and relationship with your children for years to come.

Think of divorce resolution like choosing your route during rush hour. You can take the highway (litigation), the side roads (mediation), the scenic route with professional guides (collaborative divorce), or let someone else make the decisions (arbitration). Each approach gets you to the same destination eventually, but the journey varies dramatically.

The key insight most men miss: **98% of divorce cases settle before trial, yet many men choose the most expensive and stressful path to reach that inevitable settlement.** Your job is to pick the approach that matches your specific situation, not your emotions.

ROUTE ONE: MEDIATION - THE SMART SIDE ROAD

Mediation involves hiring a neutral third party — usually a trained attorney or mental health professional — to assist you and your spouse in reaching agreements on custody, support, and property division. The mediator does not make decisions; they help guide both of you through the issues that need to be resolved.

The Real Numbers: Mediated divorces cost an average of $3,000-$7,000 total and are resolved within 3–6 months. More importantly, you control the outcomes and timeline rather than surrendering that power to strangers in court.

Success Story: David

This fellow chose mediation after his 16-year marriage ended due to growing apart. "We were both sad about the divorce, but we weren't angry at each other," he explains. "We had two teenagers who needed stability, and fighting in court would have made everything harder for them. The mediator helped us work through the financial details systematically. We kept our house sale simple, agreed on joint custody, and I was able to move on with my life without destroying our co-parenting relationship. Total cost was $4,200, and we were done in four months."

David's success wasn't luck — it was the result of calculated decisions. He recognized that his situation didn't require warfare, just professional guidance to navigate the technicalities of divorce.

ROUTE TWO: COLLABORATIVE DIVORCE - PROFESSIONAL SUPPORT WITHOUT COMBAT

Collaborative divorce is like mediation but with added support and training wheels. Each person has their own specially trained attorney, along with a team that often includes financial advisors, child specialists, and communication coaches. Everyone signs an agreement stating that if the process breaks down and litigation becomes necessary, all professionals must withdraw. This arrangement creates a strong incentive for everyone to work toward making collaboration successful, while ensuring each person receives independent legal advice throughout the process.

When Collaborative Divorce Works Best: In complex situations that require professional guidance, but where both parties want to maintain dignity and privacy. It costs more than mediation ($13,500-$27,000 total) but offers structured support for managing complicated financial or parenting issues.

Success Story: Marcus and Jennifer

They chose collaborative divorce after 14 years of marriage, when Marcus's business valuation raised complex issues regarding asset division. "We needed professional help to understand the tax implications and fair value of the business," Marcus explains. "But we didn't want to fight about it. The collaborative team included a business valuator, tax advisor, and two attorneys who worked together instead of against each other. We resolved everything in seven months with a plan that protected both our interests and our kids' college funds."

The key advantage of collaborative divorce is professional guidance within a cooperative framework. You get expert advice, minus the adversarial positioning.

ROUTE THREE: ARBITRATION - OUTSOURCING THE DECISION

Arbitration means hiring a neutral decision-maker — typically an experienced family law attorney or retired judge — to hear both sides, then make binding decisions about your case. Think of it as private court with an expert judge who actually understands family law.

Why Choose Arbitration: Most family court judges have never handled a family law case before becoming judges. So, while they might be former prosecutors, real estate attorneys, or government lawyers learning family law on the job, arbitrators are specialists who deeply understand the nuances of custody, support, and asset division.

Arbitration costs more than mediation, but less than full litigation, and you control the timeline. Instead of waiting 18 months for a trial date, you can typically resolve things within 6–9 months.

When Arbitration Makes Sense: When you need expert decision-making but want to avoid the costs and delays of traditional litigation. It works well for specific disputes — like the ambiguity of business valuation or complex custody issues — where both parties prefer an expert opinion over negotiations.

ROUTE FOUR: LITIGATION - WHEN YOU NEED COURT PROTECTION

Traditional litigation means each person hires their own attorney, files papers with the court, and lets a judge make final decisions about their family's future. This approach costs the most, takes the longest, and offers you the least control over outcomes.

The Hard Numbers: Litigated divorces cost between $15,000 and $30,000 per spouse and take 12–18 months, on average, to complete. Hidden costs include expert witnesses ($2,000-$50,000), lost wages from court appearances ($1,000-$5,000), and therapy for your family ($2,000-$10,000).

When Litigation Is Necessary: When your spouse refuses to participate in other processes, when you need court orders for immediate protection, when complex discovery is required to find hidden assets, when domestic violence or substance abuse creates safety issues, or when power imbalances make negotiation impossible.

Cautionary Tale: Matt

This guy learned litigation's limitations during his two-year custody battle. "I thought the judge would see that I'd been the primary caretaker when my wife traveled for work," he explained. "Instead, I got fifteen minutes to explain fifteen years of parenting. The judge awarded her primary custody because she made less money and could 'provide stability.' I now see my kids every other weekend, and it cost me $38,000 to lose."

Matt's story highlights a key issue in litigation: judges make lasting decisions about your family based on limited information presented during brief court appearances.

THE DECISION FRAMEWORK THAT CHANGES EVERYTHING

Your choice of process should match your specific circumstances, not your emotions about the divorce. Use this strategic framework to evaluate your best option:

Communication Reality Check: Can you and your spouse have a conversation about practical matters without it becoming a screaming match? If yes, mediation or collaborative approaches can work. If not, you might need litigation's structure.

Financial Transparency Test: Do you have access to the financial information needed to make informed decisions? Has either spouse been secretive about money or business dealings? Mediation requires mutual transparency, while litigation provides formal discovery tools.

Safety and Trust Assessment: Are there safety concerns that need court intervention? Has your spouse made false accusations or shown patterns of manipulation? High-conflict situations often require the protective measures of litigation.

Complexity Evaluation: Is your situation straightforward (W-2 jobs, simple assets, clear custody preferences) or complex (business ownership, multiple properties, complicated custody issues)? Simple situations favor mediation, while complex scenarios might benefit from collaborative divorce.

Priority Clarification: What matters most to you — speed, cost, privacy, control, or comprehensive protection? Different approaches serve different priorities.

Sam used this framework when his wife of twelve years asked for a divorce. "Honestly, I was hurt and angry," he admits. "My first instinct was to hire the most aggressive attorney I could find. But when I really evaluated our situation, she wasn't trying to screw me over — she just wasn't happy anymore. We could still talk about our kids without fighting, and she had never been dishonest about money. Mediation saved us both money and preserved our ability to co-parent."

YOUR CHILDREN ARE WATCHING

Whatever you decide, your children will observe how you handle this crisis. Years from now, do you want them to remember that you chose the path that preserved their college fund and minimized conflict... or that you spent their inheritance fighting about who gets the china cabinet?

To be clear, litigation isn't evil — sometimes it's necessary protection — but make sure you're choosing it based on your situation's requirements, not because you're angry or want to punish your spouse.

SHIELD YOURSELF: THE STRATEGIC ASSESSMENT

Before making this critical decision, honestly answer these questions:

Communication Assessment: Rate your ability to discuss practical divorce matters with your spouse without resorting to personal attacks (1–10 scale). Scores of 6 or higher suggest mediation potential.

Financial Transparency: Do you have access to complete financial information? Has your spouse been secretive about money, business dealings, or spending? Transparency is essential for mediation success.

Safety Evaluation: Are there safety concerns, threats of false allegations, or patterns of manipulation? These factors usually require litigation's protective structure.

Complexity Factor: Rate your situation's complexity (1–10 scale, with simple assets and clear preferences = 1, multiple businesses and contested custody = 10). Higher levels of complexity often benefit from professional support.

Professional Assessment: What type of attorney has your spouse hired? Collaborative attorneys suggest cooperation potential, while "shark" attorneys tear into the litigation process.

Your answers should identify the best path forward. If communication remains effective, finances are transparent, no safety issues exist, and both parties seek a quick resolution, mediation provides great value. If the situation is more complex but both sides are committed to fairness, a collaborative divorce with professional support in a cooperative framework is appropriate. If power imbalances, deception, or safety concerns are present, litigation may be your only protection.

ONE MOVE THAT MATTERS

This week, have one honest conversation — either with your spouse directly or through attorneys — about whether you can resolve this through mediation. Even if you're not sure mediation will work, ask. You might be surprised by the answer.

The worst they can say is no, and you're no worse off than right now if they do. The best outcome is avoiding a year-long battle and saving $40,000, all while preserving your relationship with your children. Choose your battlefield based on your specific situation, not your emotions. Most battles can be won without going to war.

―――

Key Takeaways: Your choice of resolution process often determines your outcomes more than the specific issues you're fighting about. Mediation works for most cases when both parties commit to the process, while litigation is necessary when you need court protection or formal discovery powers. Your decision here will determine your timeline, costs, stress level, and relationship with your children for years to come.

―――

CHAPTER 7
WHEN DIVORCE STAYS CIVIL

You've learned how to prepare for war. You understand when litigation might be your only option. Now, you need to know something most divorce books won't tell you: most divorces don't have to turn into battles. In fact, the smartest strategy might be to keep things civil.

This doesn't mean being a pushover. This doesn't mean ignoring the Four Pillars or skipping preparation. It means understanding that sometimes the best way to protect your interests is through collaboration, not combat.

Chapter 6 showed you the cost differences of the various approaches. This chapter shows you how to execute a civil divorce strategy when it fits your situation.

BEYOND BASIC MEDIATION: THE COLLABORATIVE ADVANTAGE

You already know a little about mediation from Chapter 6 and how it bridges the gap between mediation and full litigation. We're going to dive more deeply into it here.

As a reminder, collaborative divorce is like mediation with professional backup. Each person has their own attorney, but these attorneys are specially trained to work together instead of butt horns. Think of it as a team approach, where everyone's goal is reaching a fair resolution, not winning points.

A collaborative divorce attorney explained it this way: "Collaborative divorce is an out-of-court, no-court process. The lawyers don't go to court. We don't threaten to go to court. It's a non-adversarial process that allows couples to emerge healthy and wholehearted instead of bitter and resentful."

During a collaborative divorce, everyone signs an agreement that if the process fails and you end up in litigation, all the collaborative professionals must withdraw. This creates a shared incentive to make it work. Your attorney can't secretly hope for litigation, because they'd lose the case entirely.

The process includes built-in protections for both sides. You don't allow stonewalling and stalling, but you provide enough space for emotional adjustment. Remember, often one person has been thinking about divorce for up to a year before they speak up, while the other person feels blindsided. This approach gives you time to make good decisions without being rushed by court deadlines. You get to set your own timeline based on your family's needs, not a judge's calendar.

REAL STORY: HOW PAUL DID IT RIGHT (MOSTLY)

Paul's story shows both the benefits and challenges of trying to keep things amicable. When he and his wife decided they were done, he reached out to attorneys with a clear message: "We agree that we're done. We're not going to fight about a bunch of stuff. I know that it comes down to money and time with the kids."

His approach was strategic from day one. He didn't want to rock the boat too much, which is how many men feel. He just wanted to get through the process as quickly as possible, spend as little money as possible, and still get a good product—an agreement that was clear, concise, and actually said what he thought it said.

Paul's divorce started amicably and remained so throughout most of the process. They sorted out custody arrangements, financial support, and asset division without much drama. His ex-wife earned more than he did, but he didn't pursue spousal support. They agreed to a 50–50 custody arrangement. The whole process was wrapped up fairly quickly and cost-effectively.

Paul's story becomes more interesting six months after the divorce was finalized. His ex-wife hired a new attorney and attempted to relitigate several issues. She accused him of putting the kids in danger by reporting legitimate safety concerns to child protective services. She was upset about schedule changes and challenged the educational decisions he made for the kids.

They ended up in mediation for four hours, accomplished nothing, and eventually the whole thing just faded away. But it cost Paul time, money, and stress that could have been avoided with more specific language in the original agreement.

The key insight: even in amicable divorces, preparation and detailed agreements still matter. Being civil doesn't mean being careless.

THE MINDSET THAT MAKES IT WORK

Successful collaborative divorce requires a specific mindset. As one expert put it, "Mindset is the most important part of achieving a successful divorce. A successful divorce means that you've come out of the process not feeling like you're broken."

No one ever loves how a divorce is resolved. If you're going to have to pay money to your ex-spouse, sure, you're not going to enjoy paying it. If you don't get to see your kids as often as you'd like, you won't love that either. But it's about being reasonably content. It's about feeling like you were at least heard, received a fair resolution, and were part of the process of reaching it.

This means accepting some responsibility for your contribution to the marriage's end. It means making amends, where appropriate and safe to do so, and having some emotional closure so that you're not that couple duking it out in family court for years while your children suffer.

The collaborative process model's non-defensive communication approach teaches you to say things like "say what you mean, mean what you say, but don't say it mean." They encourage responses like "you might be right" or "let me think about it" instead of immediately defending your position.

This isn't about being weak. It's about being smart enough to recognize that sometimes de-escalation gets you better results than escalation.

WHEN CIVIL APPROACHES DON'T WORK

Some situations make a peaceful resolution almost impossible. If your spouse has a personality disorder that hinders rational negotiation, if there's domestic violence that creates safety concerns or a power imbalance, if assets are hidden and you need court-ordered discovery, if your spouse refuses to provide basic financial information, or if one party is entirely unwilling to compromise on anything, then litigation might be your only option.

Don't force a collaborative process when the situation calls for protective action. Remember the Four Pillars: if you can't protect your money, children, freedom, or sanity through collaboration, you need to shift strategies. But before assuming your situation calls for war, honestly evaluate whether a peaceful solution is possible. This isn't about whether you like your spouse or trust them completely. It's about whether you can work together to resolve practical issues in a structured setting with professional guidance.

BUILDING YOUR COLLABORATIVE TEAM

Decided to pursue a collaborative approach? Great, now building the right team is crucial. Look for attorneys who are specifically trained in collaborative law. These aren't just regular attorneys who say they "do" collaborative divorce. They're professionals who have completed specialized training and are part of collaborative practice groups.

Collaborative attorneys work in networks where they refer to and trust one another, remaining supportive rather than combative. As a collaborative attorney explained to me, "This is the crazy, radical thing about collaborative — the lawyers actually trust each other to collaborate in a good way on behalf of the client. We don't have to worry that, if we make a mistake, our collaborative colleague will use it against us. They're going to point it out and be like, 'hey, did you notice you missed a zero?'"

Your team might also include a financial neutral. This is someone who can analyze different settlement scenarios, help you understand the actual costs of keeping certain assets, create realistic post-divorce budgets, and identify tax implications of various settlement options.

Mental health professionals might also be included to support communication, co-parenting planning, and healthy processing of the emotional fallout of divorce.

The cost is usually at least twice that of mediation, but still much less than litigation. Think of it as insurance — you receive professional advocacy and legal protection while staying efficient.

MAKING THE PITCH TO YOUR SPOUSE

If collaborative divorce works for your situation, timing and presentation are important when bringing up the idea. Ideally, you should introduce the concept when you announce your intent to divorce.

The pitch sounds like this: "I've spoken to a collaborative lawyer, and there's a way to do this so we don't ruin each other's lives. We're going to be able to demonstrate resilience in the face of adversity to our children. We're not going to ruin our kids. Let's at least agree to that."

If your spouse has already hired a traditional litigation attorney, you can still suggest obtaining a second opinion. Most collaborative lawyers will provide a list of other collaborative attorneys for your spouse to interview. Again, they work in practice groups where members refer to one another and function as teams.

You can frame it as your final request: "Could you please at least do me one courtesy as my final gift, my final ask before we separate for the rest of our lives? Can we at least try? Would you at least keep an open mind and go talk to a collaboratively trained attorney and see if you like that process?"

Most people will at least consider this option, unless there's active abuse, active addiction, serious, untreated mental health issues, or financial fraud that requires court intervention.

DOCUMENTATION STILL MATTERS

Even in a collaborative divorce, you still need to follow the Four Pillars. You still need to document everything. You still need to gather financial records. You still need to protect your relationship with your children. You still need to avoid saying or doing things that could be used against you later.

However, you're using this information to negotiate fairly rather than to attack. You're protecting yourself while working toward a resolution rather than a victory.

Keep thorough records of agreements made during the process. Record any changes to temporary arrangements. Keep your custody journal up to date. Follow all the preparation steps from earlier chapters, but use them as tools for settlement rather than tools of conflict.

SHIELD YOURSELF: THE CIVIL DIVORCE ASSESSMENT

Before committing to a collaborative or mediation process, honestly evaluate your situation using these questions:

Can you and your spouse have a conversation about practical matters without it descending into a screaming match?

Does your spouse provide basic financial information when you ask for it?

Are both of you willing to compromise on some issues to avoid the cost and stress of litigation?

Is your relationship free of domestic violence, serious substance abuse, or untreated mental health issues that create power imbalances?

Do you both want to minimize the impact on your children and preserve some ability to co-parentNone?

Are you both more concerned with reaching a fair resolution than with "winning" or punishing each other?

If you answered yes to most of these questions, collaborative approaches might work. If not, you might need to consider more protective strategies.

Don't convince yourself that collaboration will succeed if the basic dynamics make it impossible. But also, don't assume you have to fight if there's a reasonable path to resolution.

ONE MOVE THAT MATTERS

This week, research collaborative attorneys in your area. Look for lawyers who are members of collaborative practice groups, not just those who say they "do" collaborative work. Interview at least two collaborative attorneys to understand how the process works and whether it might fit your situation. Even if you ultimately decide on a different approach, understanding all your options helps you make strategic decisions rather than emotional ones.

Most collaborative attorneys provide initial consultations to help you determine if the process fits your situation. They're not trying to sell you on collaboration if it's not suitable — they aim for successful outcomes, which depend on honest evaluations of whether peaceful resolution is achievable for their clients.

Key Takeaways: Calculated decisions beats emotional reactions. Sometimes the smartest move is collaboration, not combat. Keep your powder dry, but don't start shooting if you don't have to. The goal is protecting your interests, not proving who's right.

CHAPTER 8
MASTERING THE CUSTODY CHESS GAME

If you have children, this is the single most important chapter in this book.

Everything else — money, property, even your own happiness — is secondary to your relationship with your kids.

The following is worth repeating here, since most fathers don't understand it: custody battles aren't won by being a good father. They're won by being able to prove you're a good father in ways that family court judges understand and value. That is what will determine whether you get equal time with your children or become a weekend visitor.

THE BRUTAL REALITY FOR FATHERS

Time for some straight talk about custody.

More fathers are getting equal custody than ever before — that's the good news. Courts are increasingly recognizing that children benefit from meaningful relationships with both parents.

But here's the part that stings: you still have to fight for it —and fight smart.

Traditional assumptions die hard. Many judges, lawyers, and custody evaluators still operate with unconscious biases when it comes to parenting roles. You can't just assume your parenting contributions will be recognized and valued equally.

Mothers often have a documentation advantage, since they're more likely to keep baby books, take photos, save school artwork, and generally document their children's lives. This creates a paper trail that can be spun as greater involvement to a court.

The concept of the "primary caregiver" still holds significant influence in many courts. They often attempt to identify one parent as the "primary caregiver" and allocate more time with the children to that parent. You need to demonstrate that you've been an equal caregiver or at least show that equal custody is in your children's best interests.

A harsh reality that nobody wants to tell you is that love doesn't win custody cases. Documentation does.

TWO DADS, SAME LOVE, COMPLETELY DIFFERENT OUTCOMES

Mark and Sam - two incredible fathers. Both went through a divorce. Both wanted equal custody of their kids. But their outcomes couldn't have been more different.

Mark coached his daughter's soccer team for three years, never missed a school play, and absolutely rocked bedtime stories every night... he even did the voices! Everyone who knew him would testify that he was a devoted dad. But when custody was decided, he got every other weekend.

Why? His wife had kept a detailed journal of her daily parenting activities. She had photos of herself at every school event. She saved every piece of artwork and report card.

Mark had... his memories, and the testimony of a few friends.

The court didn't doubt that Mark loved his daughter. But his wife had evidence of her involvement, while Mark only had stories about his.

The painful lesson: In family court, if you didn't document it, it didn't happen.

Compare that to Sam, who started his parenting journal the day he suspected divorce was on the horizon. He documented everything: every school pickup and drop-off, every doctor's appointment he attended, every bedtime routine he handled, every homework session he supervised, every meal he prepared, every extracurricular activity he attended.

He took photos at school events. He saved emails with teachers. He kept receipts for children's expenses he paid.

When custody was evaluated, Sam could prove his daily involvement with specific dates, times, and activities. His documentation showed a clear pattern of equal parenting that had been going on for months. Even more, his children knew how involved he was.

The result: Sam got exactly the 50/50 custody arrangement he wanted.

The lesson: Documentation turns your love into evidence.

BUILDING YOUR CUSTODY CASE: THE DOCUMENTATION SYSTEM

Look, I get it. "Journaling" sounds like something your wife does, not you.

But we're not talking about writing poetry about your feelings or star sign here. We're talking about creating evidence that will determine whether you see your kids every day or every other weekend. Start documenting everything today. Use any system that works for you — phone notes, journal, calendar app — but stay consistent.

Every day, log the times you pick up or drop off your children, the activities you do together, the meals you serve, how you assist with homework, your bedtime routines, and any concerns or issues. You don't need to write a detailed report —open your calendar app and make simple notes: "Took kids to school today. Helped with math homework. Bedtime stories." That's it. Keep it straightforward, consistent, and effective.

On a weekly basis, you should track school events you attended, extracurricular activities, doctor and dentist appointments, playdates you arranged, and special activities or outings. Monthly, document school conferences, major purchases for your children, changes in your children's behavior or needs, and communication with teachers or other professionals.

THE PHOTO STRATEGY THAT ACTUALLY WORKS

Pictures tell stories that words can't. But you need the right kinds of photos to build your case.

Your kids will always look cute, but that's not the main goal here. Good photos in this context show you actively involved with your children — reading, playing, helping. Take pictures of yourself at school or extracurricular events, during family activities and outings, and during regular daily routines like meals, homework, and bedtime.

Avoid photos that only show you and the kids smiling at the camera, as they don't demonstrate involvement. Also, while we're discussing photographic evidence, steer clear of party photos that could be misinterpreted, pictures with alcohol visible, or any images that could be taken out of context.

BUILDING YOUR CHILDREN'S SUPPORT NETWORK

Courts pay attention to which parent has relationships with which people in children's lives. If you don't know your children's teachers, coaches, doctors, and friends' parents, start building those relationships now.

Introduce yourself to teachers at the start of the school year. Attend parent-teacher conferences. Make sure you're on the school's email list. Volunteer for field trips or classroom activities. Joining the Parent-Teacher Organization or Association is a great way to get involved. You don't have to become co-President of the PTO like I did, but consider volunteering to lead a committee, handing out snacks at lunch, or helping decorate for the school dance. Get involved!

For medical providers, make sure you're listed as a contact. Attend appointments whenever possible. Know your children's medical history, medications, and concerns.

Attend practices with coaches and activity leaders (such as band, orchestra, choir, drama, debate, etc.), not just games, concerts, or matches. Volunteer to support the team, like through the booster club. Build relationships with other parents.

These individuals will serve as your witnesses. When a custody evaluator questions the teacher about which parent is involved, you want your name to come up naturally and positively.

HANDLING FALSE ALLEGATIONS

False allegations of abuse, neglect, or substance abuse can destroy your case before you even get to defend yourself.

Protect yourself proactively by never being alone with your spouse during exchanges. Use public places with cameras. Document any threats or false claims she makes. Keep evidence of your normal, healthy parenting. If she has a history of instability or false claims, document them too.

If false allegations are made, don't panic or retaliate. Contact your attorney immediately. Gather evidence that disproves the claims — text messages, witnesses, documentation of your activities. Follow all court orders, even temporary ones based on false claims. Fighting them the wrong way makes things worse.

WORKING WITH CUSTODY EVALUATORS

If your case involves a custody evaluator or Guardian Ad Litem (GAL), know that this person has significant influence because they make recommendations that judges usually follow.

Prepare for the evaluation by organizing your documentation in chronological order. Develop a parenting plan proposal that demonstrates you've considered the details. Collect character references from teachers, coaches, and others who have observed your parenting. Ensure your home is ready for a visit — clean and safe — so it clearly serves as an appropriate space for children.

During the evaluation, be honest but strategic. Don't criticize your ex. Instead, focus on your strengths as a parent. Offer specific examples of your involvement rather than making broad statements. Show that you support your children's relationship with their mother. Prove that you can co-parent effectively.

THE PARENTING PLAN THAT WINS

Courts love parents who come prepared with detailed, child-focused proposals. Don't just ask for "joint custody" — present a specific plan that shows you've thought through the logistics of how that would work. That looks like a regular parenting schedule with specific days and times, holiday and vacation schedules, transportation arrangements, communication between homes, decision-making for education, medical, and religious matters, and how you'll handle future disagreements.

The more detailed and reasonable your proposal, the more likely you are to get what you want. Courts appreciate fathers who come with realistic, detailed proposals rather than vague demands for "fair treatment."

SHIELD YOURSELF: TOM'S 50/50 VICTORY

Tom's wife filed for divorce when their twins were eight years old, immediately demanding primary custody and limiting Tom's time to every other weekend.

Tom's response was methodical.

- Month one, he started detailed documentation of all parenting activities.
- Month two, he increased his involvement in school activities and sports.
- Month three, he built relationships with teachers, coaches, and other parents.

- Month four, he took parenting classes to demonstrate commitment.
- Month five, he created a detailed parenting plan proposal.
- Month six, he prepared a comprehensive evidence package for court.

The result: Tom got exactly the 50/50 schedule he wanted. The judge commented that his preparation and documentation were the most thorough she'd ever seen.

"I realized I couldn't just be a good dad," Tom says. "I had to prove I was a good dad. The documentation made all the difference."

TOOLS FOR HIGH-CONFLICT SITUATIONS

If you're dealing with a high-conflict situation, there are extra tools you can use. In many states, parenting coordinators are authorized to make decisions that can only be overturned by a judge. When you face disagreements and someone says things like, "I'm not going to agree to this, I'm not going to agree to that, I'm not going to let our son play soccer," you'll have someone to serve as the referee and make the call.

Use structured communication tools, such as Our Family Wizard, to keep all parenting exchanges professional and documented. If your children are having a hard time with the divorce, getting them therapy offers both support and professional insight into their needs.

THE BOTTOM LINE ON CUSTODY

Winning custody as a father isn't about being perfect. It's about being prepared. It's about understanding that love alone isn't enough — you need evidence.

Fathers who gain equal custody treat the process as a serious matter. They document everything, foster relationships, and present their case professionally.

They understand that their children's future depends on getting this right. And they're willing to do whatever it takes to be the fathers their children need, both during and after the divorce.

ONE MOVE THAT MATTERS

This week, set up your parenting documentation system. Select your preferred method (such as a calendar app, journal, or notes app) and record every interaction with your children for the upcoming seven days. Include times, activities, and any notable moments. Print or screenshot your first week's records as proof that you're serious about this.

Your children are counting on you to get this right. Don't let them down because you weren't prepared to prove what they already know — that you're a fantastic father.

Start documenting today. Your future relationship with your children depends on it.

Key Takeaways: Fathers can win equal custody with proper preparation. Love doesn't win custody cases — evidence does. Documentation, relationship building with your children's "people," and strategically presenting your parenting capabilities are essential for achieving a custody arrangement in your children's best interests.

CHAPTER 9
SURVIVING HIGH-CONFLICT DIVORCE

Remember Adam, from Chapter 1, who thought he knew his wife? Sure, she'd always been dramatic and prone to mood swings, but he figured that was just her quirky personality. Over the years, he'd learned to manage her emotions, avoid certain topics, and keep the peace for the sake of their two daughters.

In case you forgot what this poor guy went through, within 48 hours, his wife filed for divorce, obtained a restraining order claiming he was abusive, and told their daughters that he was dangerous, even though he never laid a hand on his wife or children. He had never even raised his voice in anger, but suddenly he was locked out of his own home, unable to see his kids, and facing criminal charges that could ruin his career.

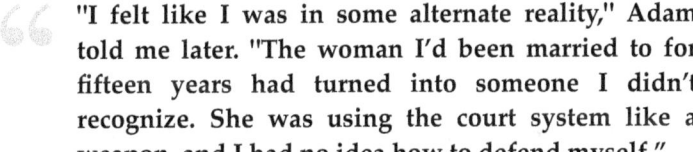

"I felt like I was in some alternate reality," Adam told me later. "The woman I'd been married to for fifteen years had turned into someone I didn't recognize. She was using the court system like a weapon, and I had no idea how to defend myself."

Adam wasn't facing a typical divorce. He was facing a high-conflict one, thanks to his spouse's personality disorder traits, which caused her to regard divorce not as the end of a relationship, but as the ultimate battleground for control and revenge.

Sounds familiar? Then this chapter could save you years of heartache and hundreds of thousands of dollars.

RECOGNIZING HIGH-CONFLICT PERSONALITIES EARLY

High-conflict spouses don't behave like normal people going through a tough patch. They have fundamentally different motivations and use tactics that seem irrational to mentally healthy individuals. The sooner you understand what you're dealing with, the better you can protect yourself and your children.

The Four Core Traits

Emotional Dysregulation: They experience intense emotions that are disproportionate to the situation. Small disagreements explode into major crises. They can't self-soothe or calm down once triggered. Their emotional state determines their reality, not facts or logic.

Sarah, whose ex-husband had narcissistic traits, described it this way: "He could go from zero to rage in seconds over something like me asking about his day. Then he'd act like I was crazy for being upset about his reaction."

Black-and-White Thinking: Everything is either perfect or terrible, with no middle ground. You're either completely good or completely evil in their eyes. They can't hold nuanced perspectives or see situations from multiple angles.

Blame and Projection: Nothing is ever their fault. They project their behaviors onto others and genuinely believe their own distorted version of events and often accuse others of exactly what they're doing themselves.

Control and Manipulation: They need to control outcomes and other people's behaviors. When normal means of influence don't work, they escalate to manipulation, threats, and using institutions like courts or child protective services as weapons.

Early Warning Signs During Marriage

Looking back, most men realize the signs were there long before divorce — walking on eggshells to avoid triggering their anger, having conversations where they felt like they were going crazy because their version of events didn't match reality, being blamed for their emotional reactions or behavioral problems. Their friends or family members often express concern about how their spouse treats them. They find themselves making excuses for their partner's behavior or avoiding social situations because of mood swings. Feeling like they are managing their partner's emotions more than living their own lives.

The Divorce Trigger

For high-conflict personalities, divorce isn't just the end of a relationship - it's the ultimate narcissistic injury. Their overwhelming need for control, their black-and-white thinking, and their inability to regulate emotions all spin up a perfect storm of destructive behavior.

They often view divorce as a battle they must win at all costs, even if winning means harming the children, draining both parties financially, or making everyone miserable for years. Typical ideas like compromise, acting in the best interests of the children, or moving on with life are not part of their thinking.

SPECIFIC DOCUMENTATION STRATEGIES FOR FALSE ALLEGATIONS

High-conflict spouses frequently make false allegations as a strategic tool. Sadly, even false accusations of abuse, violence, substance problems, or child endangerment can give them immediate tactical advantages in custody and support decisions. Your best defense is to document before allegations are made.

The Preemptive Documentation System

Start documenting concerning behaviors immediately, even if you're not sure divorce is coming. The behavior of those with high-conflict personalities often escalates before they leave, and having a paper trail of their actions will protect you when they start rewriting history.

Keep a detailed journal with dates, times, witnesses, and objective descriptions of incidents. Focus on behaviors, not your emotional reactions. Instead of "She was acting crazy," write "She threw a plate at the wall, called me a [specific words], and told the children I was a bad father. Children present: Sara (age 8) and Tommy (age 6). Incident lasted approximately 20 minutes."

Audio and Video Evidence

If you live in a one-party consent state, record interactions whenever possible. Many phones have apps that can record calls or conversations with the press of a button. Be familiar with the functionality of yours, and with your state's recording laws and follow them exactly.

Video evidence can be especially powerful. Security cameras in common areas of your home can capture threatening behavior, property damage, or concerning interactions with children. Doorbell cameras record entries and exits that might contradict claims about your behavior.

Marcus, who successfully defended himself against false allegations, told me: "The recordings saved my case. When she claimed I threatened her, I had audio of the actual conversation where she threatened me. When she said I was never involved with the kids, I had video of me helping with homework every night."

Written Communication Only

Once you recognize you're dealing with a high-conflict personality, it's time to switch to written communication only. This means text messages or emails for all discussions about children, schedules, finances, or divorce issues.

Written communication serves three purposes:

- Prevents misunderstandings about what was actually said.
- Creates evidence of their behavior and your reasonable responses.
- Forces them to think before communicating, which often reduces impulsive and aggressive behavior.

When they try to drag you into phone arguments or face-to-face confrontations, respond with: "I want to make sure I understand you correctly. Please send me an email explaining what you'd like to discuss, and I'll respond in writing."

The Witness Strategy

Never be alone with a high-conflict spouse once divorce proceedings start. This is essential for shielding yourself from false claims of threats, violence, or inappropriate conduct.

Meet at neutral locations for all child exchanges, preferably with witnesses or security cameras. Many police stations have designated areas for custody exchanges. Shopping center parking lots, libraries, and schools also serve as natural witnesses and are often equipped with security cameras.

When you need to be in the family home, have a witness present. This could be a family member, friend, or even a hired professional supervisor. The goal is to ensure that credible witnesses can immediately refute any accusations.

COMMUNICATION TECHNIQUES THAT DON'T TRIGGER ESCALATION

Communicating with high-conflict personalities requires a completely different set of strategies. In fact, standard advice like "talking things through" or "expressing your feelings" often worsens situations by giving them emotional ammunition.

The BIFF Method

BIFF stands for Brief, Informative, Friendly, and Firm. This communication style gives high-conflict personalities no emotional hooks to grab onto, while maintaining your professionalism and protecting your legal position.

Brief: Keep all communications as short as possible. Long explanations give them more material to twist and argue about. State your point. Then stop talking.

Informative: Stick to factual information about schedules, logistics, or children's needs. Avoid opinions, feelings, or explanations about your motivations.

Friendly: Maintain a professional, business-like tone. Don't match their emotional intensity or get dragged into arguments. Think customer service representative, not emotional spouse.

Firm: Don't negotiate everything or constantly accommodate their demands. State your position clearly and don't keep rehashing the same issues.

Example of BIFF Communication:

Instead of: "I can't believe you're trying to change the schedule again! This is the third time this month, and it's really affecting the kids. Don't you care about their stability? I've already made plans, and it's not fair to keep doing this to everyone."

Use: "I'm not available to switch weekends. The children will be ready for pickup at 6 PM Friday, as scheduled."

Gray Rock Method

The Gray Rock method involves making yourself as dull and unengaging as possible during interactions. High-conflict personalities thrive on emotional reactions, drama, and chaos. When you become emotionally unavailable, they often lose interest in targeting you.

This involves giving minimal responses to their attempts to stir drama. They'll probably explore all kinds of angles, but don't get involved. Don't defend yourself against false accusations right away. Don't try to make them see your point. Don't engage with their emotional triggers.

Respond to practical questions about children or logistics, but ignore attempts to pull you into arguments about the past, their feelings, or blame-based conversations.

Boundaries With Consequences

High-conflict personalities will constantly test boundaries and escalate when boundaries aren't enforced. You need clear boundaries with specific consequences that you're willing and able to enforce.

Examples: "If you arrive more than 15 minutes late for pickup without notice, the visit will be rescheduled."

"If you send more than three non-emergency emails per day, I will only respond to the first three."

"If you call me names or use profanity in communications, I will end the conversation immediately."

See how the key is only setting boundaries you can actually enforce and then following through consistently? Otherwise, you'll only make the situation worse by teaching them that your boundaries aren't solid and therefore don't matter.

WORKING WITH PROFESSIONALS WHO UNDERSTAND PERSONALITY DISORDERS

Not all family law professionals understand high-conflict personalities or know how to effectively handle them. Working with an attorney, mediator, or mental health professional who lacks this knowledge can therefore exacerbate your situation.

Attorney Selection for High-Conflict Cases

Specific experience with high-conflict divorces and personality disorders is vital. They should understand that normal negotiation tactics don't work, and that aggressive pushback often escalates the situation.

Ask potential attorneys: "What's your experience with high-conflict spouses and personality disorders?"

"How do you handle cases involving false allegations?"

"What's your approach when mediation isn't appropriate?"

The right attorney will understand the need for extensive documentation, will know how to present evidence of the other party's behavior to courts, and will have strategies for protecting you during the process.

Mental Health Professionals

Work with a therapist who understands trauma and high-conflict relationships and can help you process what you've experienced, but without minimizing it or pushing you toward premature forgiveness.

Many therapists don't understand the dynamics of high-conflict divorces. They may give well-meaning advice that's actually quite dangerous, like "try to work things out" or "don't document everything because it looks vindictive."

Guardian ad Litem and Custody Evaluators

These professionals have enormous influence over custody decisions. Some are well-trained in recognizing manipulation and high-conflict behaviors, while others can be easily manipulated by convincing high-conflict spouses.

Provide these professionals with your documentation but do so through your attorney. Remain factual and professional in all interactions. Don't attempt to diagnose your spouse or use psychological terminology. Focus on observable behaviors and their impact on the children.

PROTECTING CHILDREN FROM PARENTAL ALIENATION TACTICS

High-conflict spouses often weaponize children in divorce, engaging in parental alienation tactics that can severely damage your relationship with your kids. Understanding these tactics and responding appropriately is crucial for protecting your children and preserving your relationship.

Common Alienation Tactics

Badmouthing: Constantly criticizing you to the children, sharing inappropriate details about the divorce, or blaming you for the family breakup.

Limiting Contact: Making it difficult for you to communicate with or see the children through scheduling conflicts, "forgotten" calls, or claims that the children don't want to see you.

Creating Loyalty Conflicts: Putting children in positions where they feel they must choose between parents, or making them feel guilty for enjoying time with you.

Interference: Scheduling activities during your parenting time, being late for exchanges, or calling constantly during your time with the children.

False Claims: Telling children you don't love them, don't want to see them, or are dangerous, based on fabricated incidents.

Counter-Alienation Strategies

Document Everything: Keep detailed records of all alienating behaviors with dates, witnesses, and specific examples. This documentation may be crucial for custody modifications later.

Stay Calm and Consistent: Don't react emotionally to alienation attempts, especially not in front of the children. Continue being a loving, stable parent regardless of what's happening in the background.

Don't Badmouth Back: Never criticize their mother to the children, even if she's criticizing you. This maintains your integrity and demonstrates to the children they can trust you with their feelings.

Reassure Constantly: Tell your children you love them, you'll always be their parent, and that nothing they do or say will change that. Children often feel responsible for the divorce and need constant reassurance.

Professional Intervention: Work with child psychologists who understand parental alienation. Sometimes professional intervention is necessary to help children process what they're experiencing.

Legal Protection: Some courts can order what is called 'reunification therapy,' restrict the alienating parent's behavior, or even change custody when alienation is severe. Your attorney should know how to present alienation evidence effectively.

SHIELD YOURSELF: HIGH-CONFLICT ASSESSMENT

Use this assessment to determine if you're dealing with a high-conflict spouse who will require specialized strategies:

Does your spouse blame you for most problems in the relationship and take little responsibility for their own behavior? Do they have intense emotional reactions that seem disproportionate?

Do you find yourself walking on eggshells to avoid setting them off? Do they threaten to use the children, courts, or financial systems as weapons when they don't get their way?

Do your friends or family members express concern about how your spouse treats you? Do you feel like you're constantly defending yourself, or proving you're not the person they claim you are?

Do they have a history of quick, intense relationships that ended badly with people they now label as "crazy" or "abusive"? Do they seem to have ongoing conflicts with multiple people (family, friends, coworkers, neighbors)?

If you answered yes to most of these questions, you're likely dealing with a high-conflict personality and need specialized strategies to protect yourself.

ONE MOVE THAT MATTERS

This week, initiate your high-conflict protection system. Start documenting all interactions with your spouse using objective, factual language. Implement policies that establish written communication only. Research attorneys in your area who have specific experience with high-conflict divorces and managing personality disorders.

Most importantly, begin protecting yourself right away. Don't wait for false allegations to arise before you start documenting. Don't assume that being reasonable and fair will be appreciated or returned. Start treating your divorce as the strategic challenge it is, not like a normal relationship problem.

Key Takeaways: Divorcing high-conflict spouses with personality disorders requires a completely different set of strategies. They may use the court system as a weapon, make false allegations as tactical tools, and view divorce as a war to win rather than a problem to solve. Navigating these situations demands early recognition, thorough documentation, specialized professional assistance, and communication strategies that don't feed their need for drama and control. The aim isn't to change them or make them reasonable - it's to protect yourself and your children while navigating the system they try to weaponize against you.

CHAPTER 10
FINANCIAL WARFARE AND ASSET PROTECTION

Money makes people crazy. It just does. Add divorce to the mix, and even the most rational people often make financial decisions that haunt them for decades.

You need to understand how the financial decisions you make during divorce will affect your quality of life for the rest of your life. Get this wrong, and you could be starting over financially in your 40s or 50s. Get it right, and you'll protect your future while remaining fair to your ex and your children.

THE MYTH OF 50/50 SPLIT

First, let's dispel a myth: "equitable distribution" doesn't mean "equal distribution." It means "fair" distribution, and fair doesn't always mean 50/50.

Most states use an equitable distribution model, which means courts consider various factors when dividing assets. Factors to consider include the length of the marriage, each spouse's income and earning capacity, financial and non-financial contributions to the marriage, age and health of each spouse, standard of living during the marriage, and custody arrangements for children.

This is why a wife who stayed home to raise children might receive more than 50% of the assets — she sacrificed her past earning potential for the family's benefit. I'm not judging whether it's right or wrong, just explaining how courts tend to view it.

MARITAL VS. SEPARATE PROPERTY: KNOW THE DIFFERENCE

Understanding this distinction can save you tens of thousands of dollars.

Marital property means assets acquired during the marriage, regardless of whose name is on the title. Separate property means assets owned before marriage, inherited during marriage, or received as gifts specifically to one spouse.

Sounds simple, right? Well, here's where it gets tricky — separate property can become marital property if it's commingled, meaning mixed with marital assets, or if the other spouse contributes to its increase in value.

Example: If you owned a house before marriage but your wife helped pay the mortgage or renovate it, she might have a claim to some of the equity it gained during the marriage.

Keep your separate property separate. Don't use marital funds to improve premarital assets unless you understand the consequences.

ALIMONY: THE FACTORS YOU CAN ACTUALLY CONTROL

Alimony is often the most emotionally charged financial issue in divorce. While you can't control all the factors, you can influence some of them.

In addition to courts considering the income difference between spouses, the length of the marriage, the standard of living during the marriage, each spouse's earning capacity, age, and health of each spouse, and individual contributions to the marriage, in some jurisdictions, they also include fault in the breakdown of the marriage, although that is uncommon.

To reduce alimony liability, document your wife's earning potential. If she has education, work experience, or skills that could enable her to earn more, record them. Courts won't force her to work, but they might consider her possible income if she were employed when determining support.

Don't artificially inflate your lifestyle. Living beyond your means during marriage creates a higher standard of living, which you might be forced to maintain through alimony. That BMW lease looked good during the marriage, but now it's evidence of the lifestyle she's "accustomed to."

If she's been out of the workforce, encourage her to get training or return to work. This can reduce future alimony obligations. But do this early… waiting until you file for divorce makes it look manipulative.

Also, while it may seem terrible at first, sometimes paying higher temporary alimony for a shorter time costs less than paying lower permanent alimony that lasts forever. Run the numbers.

RETIREMENT ACCOUNTS: YOUR GOLDEN YEARS, OR HER GOLDEN PARACHUTE

Retirement accounts are often the largest marital asset but dividing them can be complicated. There are 401(k)s and 403(b)s, which require a Qualified Domestic Relations Order (QDRO) to divide without tax penalties. While IRAs can be divided through a divorce decree, timing is important due to tax implications. Pensions are also complex, especially for government and union plans, because of valuation issues.

Here's a strategy to consider: keep your retirement accounts and give your wife other assets of equal value. This avoids the complexity and costs of dividing retirement accounts. You know how to manage your own retirement — do you trust her to manage her half?

THE HOUSE DECISION: KEEP, SELL, OR WALK AWAY

The family home's value is often more emotional than financial, but it's usually the largest asset. Each option for how you deal with it has downsides.

If you keep the house, you maintain stability for children and keep any future appreciation. But you take on all maintenance and tax costs, and your equity is tied up in one asset.

If you sell the house, you both receive liquid assets and divide maintenance and selling costs. However, children lose stability and you lose control over the timing.

If your wife keeps the house, the children maintain stability, and you get liquid assets from other sources. But you might pay more in support for housing costs, and you lose any future appreciation.

Strategic consideration: Can your wife actually afford the house long-term? If not, keeping it might set her up for failure, which could affect you and your children if she can't make the payments or afford to maintain it.

BUSINESS VALUATION: WHEN YOUR COMPANY BECOMES MARITAL PROPERTY

If you own a business, it's often the most complicated asset to divide. What's the business worth? How do you assign a dollar value to your personal involvement? The business might look valuable on paper but may not generate enough cash for you to buy out your wife's share. If that's the case... do you really want your ex-wife as a business partner?! Probably not.

Your strategy options include keeping the business and giving your wife other assets, selling the business and splitting the proceeds, buying out her interest over time, or having her get a percentage of future business income.

Most guys want to keep their business. That's usually the right call, but make sure you can afford to buy her out without crippling it.

HIDDEN ASSET DISCOVERY: WHEN YOUR SPOUSE PLAYS FINANCIAL HIDE AND SEEK

You already know how some spouses try to hide assets during divorce, but do you know what to look for? Sniff around for unusual cash withdrawals or deposits, new accounts or investments you weren't told about, transfers to family members or friends, overpayments to creditors that could be reversed later, and unusual business expenses or bonuses being delayed until after the divorce.

If you suspect hidden assets, you may need a forensic accountant to investigate. This costs money, but if you find significant hidden assets, it pays for itself.

TAX IMPLICATIONS: THE IRS DOESN'T CARE ABOUT YOUR FEELINGS

Divorce has major tax consequences that many people don't consider.

For divorces finalized after 2018, alimony is not deductible for the payer... while also somehow not taxable income for the recipient. This changes the math *significantly*. You're paying alimony with after-tax dollars, making it more expensive for you and more valuable to your ex.

When it comes to asset division, you can exclude up to $250,000 ($500,000 if married filing jointly) of capital gains when selling your primary residence. Also, dividing retirement accounts incorrectly can trigger immediate tax liabilities. And consider the tax basis of investments when dividing them. An account worth $180,000 with a $20,000 tax basis is not equal to an account worth $180,000 with a $90,000 tax basis.

You can file as married filing jointly for the entire tax year if you're married on December 31st, even if you separated in January.

Who gets to claim the children as dependents? This can result in thousands of dollars in tax savings. Sometimes, it makes sense for the higher-earning spouse to pay extra support in exchange for claiming the children as dependents.

POST-DIVORCE REALITY CHECK

Most men underestimate the cost of maintaining two households. Your expenses will increase significantly while your income stays the same. You'll need to budget for your own place, duplicate household items, separate utilities, potentially higher insurance costs, and increased costs associated with seeing your children.

Don't make financial decisions based on figures from your married lifestyle. Create a realistic post-divorce budget and use that to guide your settlement decisions.

UNDERSTANDING YOUR WIFE'S MOTIVATION

Your negotiation strategy should depend on what motivates your wife's decisions. If she is concerned about financial security, focus on providing stability through consistent payments and guarantees. If she is seeking revenge and aims to punish you financially, logic and fairness may not be effective. If her main concern is the children's well-being, frame your proposals around how they benefit the children.

CREATIVE SETTLEMENT STRUCTURES

Don't just think "she gets this, I get that." Sometimes, paying more upfront costs less in the long run. You can trade retirement assets for home equity or liquid assets for illiquid ones. Consider payments that adjust based on income changes or other factors. Think about different payment amounts for different time periods.

WHEN YOU NEED PROFESSIONAL HELP

You need a financial advisor for complex asset division scenarios, business valuation issues, retirement planning adjustments, tax strategy planning, and post-divorce budgeting and investment planning.

You need a forensic accountant to handle suspected hidden assets, complex business valuations, unusual financial transactions during marriage, and disputes about income or earning capacity.

You need a QDRO specialist when dividing 401(k), 403(b), or pension plans, dealing with complex government or union retirement benefits, or if multiple retirement accounts must be divided.

SHIELD YOURSELF: THE FINANCIAL REALITY ASSESSMENT

Before you make any settlement decisions, you need to understand the long-term financial implications. What will this cost you over 10, 20, or 30 years? Are you protecting your retirement security? Are you maintaining your ability to support your children? Are you being fair without being foolish?

Consider tax consequences such as who claims children as dependents, how support payments are taxed, and the capital gains effects of asset transfers. Also, think about long-term costs, not just by estimating payments over 5, 10, or 20 years but also how inflation could impact your payments and what might happen if your income changes.

Finally, evaluate how all this affects your retirement planning, whether you're protecting your retirement assets, and if you'll be able to stop working when you planned.

THE INVESTMENT MINDSET

Think of your divorce settlement as an investment in your future. The goal isn't to "win" the financial negotiation. The goal is to protect your family's financial security, including your ex-wife's, while ensuring you can rebuild and thrive in your new life.

You want to come out of divorce financially stable enough to rebuild, keep a good relationship with your children, and avoid paying support forever. Sometimes that means accepting a settlement that feels unfair now, but safeguards your long-term interests.

Remember, every dollar you spend fighting over assets is a dollar that doesn't go to you or your children. So, pick your battles based on long-term financial impact, not short-term emotional satisfaction.

ONE MOVE THAT MATTERS

This week, gather all your financial documents and create a complete picture of your marital assets and debts. Use a simple spreadsheet with three columns:

Asset/Debt
Current Value
Marital vs. Separate

This exercise will open your eyes to what's really at stake and help you make strategic decisions rather than emotional ones.

Be sure to include everything: bank accounts, retirement accounts, investment accounts, real estate, vehicles, business interests, personal property of significant value, and all debts, including mortgages, credit cards, loans, and business debts.

Once you understand the full financial situation, you can start making strategic choices about what to pursue and what to let go. You might find that the asset you're most emotionally invested in isn't worth the expense of fighting for it.

Calculated decisions beats emotional decisions every time. Protect wealth through strategy, not emotion.

Key Takeaway: Strategy, not emotion, will safeguard your wealth. The financial choices you make during divorce will impact your quality of life for many years. Understanding marital versus separate property, reducing alimony costs, protecting retirement savings, and making strategic decisions about your house and business interests can save you thousands of dollars and secure your financial future.

CHAPTER 11
WHAT YOUR WIFE'S ATTORNEY IS TELLING HER

THE INFORMATION ADVANTAGE

He had organized his finances, documented his parenting, and hired what he believed was a capable attorney. Tom thought he was ready for divorce. Six months into the process, Tom felt like he was playing chess while his wife was playing checkers — but somehow, she was still winning!

"I kept getting surprised by things," Tom recalls. "She'd make requests that seemed to come out of nowhere, but her attorney always had precedent and legal reasoning. My attorney would scramble to respond, but we were always one step behind."

Tom's experience illustrates something crucial about modern divorce: **information asymmetry often determines outcomes more than actual facts.** When one side knows the playbook and the other doesn't, the prepared side gains significant advantages.

This chapter isn't about encouraging adversarial behavior or escalating conflict. It's about **understanding common legal strategies so you can recognize them, respond appropriately, and make informed decisions** about your approach.

WHY KNOWLEDGE EQUALS PROTECTION

After representing both men and women in divorce for over two decades, I've noticed a pattern. Many attorneys provide their female clients with comprehensive strategic guidance from day one, while male clients often receive more reactive advice that focuses on responding to what's already happened.

This isn't necessarily intentional bias — it often reflects different communication styles and expectations — but the result is that men frequently find themselves responding to strategies they don't understand rather than implementing proactive approaches.

Understanding common legal strategies allows you to:

- Recognize tactical moves early, responding strategically
- Make informed decisions about your own approach
- Protect yourself from manipulation without becoming manipulative yourself
- Focus on fair resolution, maintaining appropriate boundaries

COMMON EARLY PREPARATION STRATEGIES

Most experienced divorce attorneys encourage their clients to begin careful planning well before filing papers, which typically includes several key elements that you should understand.

Documentation Strategies: Comprehensive documentation of daily life, including parenting activities, household responsibilities, and any concerning behaviors from their spouse. The goal is creating a factual record that supports their client's desired outcomes.

Financial Positioning: Strategic financial preparation might include organizing complete financial records, establishing individual banking relationships, and documenting income sources and variations. Some attorneys advise clients to be cautious about making major financial changes that could be viewed unfavorably later.

Relationship Management: Clients are often coached to maintain professional communication styles and avoid emotional reactions that could be used as evidence. This includes being mindful about social media presence and focusing on creating positive interactions when possible.

Support Network Development: Often including consulting with therapists, financial advisors, and other professionals who can provide both emotional support and expert testimony, if needed.

The Collaborative Response: Once you understand these common strategies, you can create your own approach focused on fair outcomes rather than gaining a tactical advantage. Honestly document your parenting and contributions. Handle your finances transparently. Communicate professionally. Build a support network that includes qualified professionals.

NARRATIVE DEVELOPMENT IN LEGAL STRATEGY

One of the most important concepts to understand is how legal narratives develop during divorce proceedings. Experienced attorneys know that facts alone don't determine outcomes — the story that connects them does.

Common Narrative Themes: Legal strategies often focus on themes that connect with judges and mediators. These might include showing primary caretaking responsibilities, demonstrating stability and consistency, emphasizing financial contributions or sacrifices, expressing sincere concern for children's wellbeing, and presenting the client as reasonable and cooperative.

Social Media and Public Presentation: Many attorneys warn clients to be very cautious about their social media activity during a divorce. This often involves avoiding posts that might suggest irresponsible spending, too much time socializing, or inappropriate conduct around children.

The Strategic Counter-Narrative: Rather than simply defending against negative narratives, you can proactively build your own positive alternatives that center your genuine contributions as a father and provider. Document your involvement in your children's lives without appearing calculating. Maintain consistency between your private behavior and public presentation.

FINANCIAL STRATEGY AWARENESS

Understanding common financial strategies helps you protect your interests without engaging in questionable tactics.

Income Evaluation Approaches: Some attorneys advise clients that courts will look at earning capacity, not simply current income. This might include past overtime work, professional credentials, and potential career advancement. Understanding this helps you present your financial situation accurately while avoiding underestimating your obligations.

Asset and Debt Analysis: Comprehensive financial strategy typically includes analyzing all marital assets and debts, understanding valuation methods, and identifying which items are worth fighting for and which aren't so you make strategic decisions about what matters most.

Support Calculation Factors: Many attorneys educate their clients about how support is calculated, including factors like length of marriage, income disparity, and standard of living during marriage. Understanding these factors helps you set realistic expectations and proposals.

The Collaborative Financial Approach: When you understand financial strategies, you can participate in transparent financial disclosure while still protecting your legitimate interests. Provide complete financial information willingly. Work with qualified professionals to ensure accurate valuations. Focus on building sustainable arrangements rather than jockeying for short-term advantages.

CUSTODY STRATEGY UNDERSTANDING

Custody strategies often focus on demonstrating fitness as a parent and commitment to children's best interests.

Parenting Documentation: Many attorneys advise clients to increase their visible involvement in children's activities, encouraging them to volunteer at schools, attend medical appointments, and document all parenting activities comprehensively.

Stability and Routine Emphasis: Common strategies focus on demonstrating consistency, stability, and the ability to provide structured environments for children. This might include maintaining regular schedules, creating child-friendly living spaces, and showing involvement in children's education and activities.

Co-Parenting Readiness: Attorneys often coach clients to demonstrate their ability to support the child's relationship with the other parent, communicate effectively with them about parenting issues, and prioritize children's needs over personal grievances.

The Positive Custody Response: Understanding custody strategies helps you genuinely strengthen your parenting, rather than just appearing to do so. Increase your actual involvement because it benefits your children, not just your case. Create stability because children need it, not just because it looks good in court. Prepare for effective co-parenting sincerely and earnestly because it serves your children's long-term interests.

RECOGNIZING NEGOTIATION STRATEGIES

Understanding common negotiation approaches helps you respond strategically rather than emotionally.

Anchoring and Positioning: Experienced negotiators often start with high requests, understanding they'll inevitably have to negotiate downward. This establishes a broad negotiation range and makes moderate requests seem reasonable by comparison.

Timing and Pressure Tactics: Using time pressure or your desire to "get it over with" to encourage agreement to less favorable terms.

Information Control: Controlling information flow, revealing some details while withholding others until the timing is advantageous.

Emotional Positioning: Framing one party as the victim or more reasonable party, which can influence mediators and judges.

The Strategic Response: When you understand these tactics, you can respond thoughtfully rather than reactively. Set your own reasonable timeline and stick to it. Gather complete information before making decisions. Focus on reaching fair outcomes rather than gaining emotional satisfaction. Maintain your integrity while protecting your interests.

PROTECTIVE STRATEGIES WITHOUT ESCALATION

The key to responding to methodical approaches is maintaining your own integrity while protecting your interests.

Professional Communication: Always communicate as if your words will be read in court, because they might be. Stay factual, brief, and focused narrowly on practical matters rather than emotional issues.

Strategic Documentation: Document your own positive contributions and interactions, without appearing calculated or manipulative, by creating accurate records showing you in a positive light rather than building a case against your spouse.

Boundary Setting: Set clear boundaries about acceptable behavior and communication while remaining respectful. You can be firm without being aggressive.

Collaborative Positioning: Position yourself as someone focused on fair resolution and your children's well-being. This isn't just strategy — it should reflect your genuine priorities.

SHIELD YOURSELF: STRATEGIC AWARENESS ASSESSMENT

Before the next significant interaction or decision in your divorce process, consider these questions:

Information Evaluation: What information are you sharing, and how might it be used strategically? Are you providing complete and accurate information while still protecting sensitive details appropriately?

Communication Review: How are you communicating with your spouse and her attorney? Are your messages professional, factual, and focused on reaching practical solutions?

Narrative Assessment: What story are your actions and words telling? Does this narrative support your goals for custody, finances, and future relationships?

Response Strategy: Are you responding reactively to your spouse's moves, or proactively implementing your own positive strategy?

Long-Term Perspective: Are your current approaches sustainable and likely to support a good co-parenting relationship long-term?

THE COLLABORATIVE ALTERNATIVE

Understanding methodical approaches doesn't mean you need to adopt manipulative tactics! Instead, use this knowledge to:

Make Informed Decisions: Recognize when certain approaches are being used, then respond reasonably rather than reactively.

Maintain High Standards: Hold yourself to high ethical standards while protecting your legitimate interests.

Focus on Fair Outcomes: Use calculated decisions to achieve fair resolution rather than to "win" at all costs.

Protect Your Children: Ensure that your approach protects your children's interests and preserves the possibility of healthy co-parenting.

Build Your Own Positive Case: Rather than just defending against negative narratives, tell your own positive story through documenting consistent, genuine behavior.

ONE MOVE THAT MATTERS

This week, evaluate all your recent communications and actions from a strategic perspective. What patterns have you identified? What story are your behaviors conveying? What evidence are you producing?

Then adjust your approach accordingly — not to be deceptive or manipulative, but to be strategic and protective — focusing on behaviors that genuinely serve your children's interests, while also supporting your legal position.

Knowing and countering common strategies doesn't mean resorting to questionable tactics. It means you can respond intelligently while maintaining your integrity.

Key Takeaways: Recognizing common legal strategies enables you to identify tactical moves, respond effectively, and safeguard your interests without escalating conflict or compromising your integrity. Apply this knowledge to make informed decisions and stay focused on achieving fair outcomes that benefit your family's long-term well-being.

PART FOUR
THE RESOLUTION PHASE

CHAPTER 12
NEGOTIATING FROM STRENGTH, NOT DESPERATION

Steve was a successful real estate developer who had built million-dollar properties from the ground up. But sitting across from his wife's attorney during settlement talks, he found himself making rookie mistakes that would have gotten him laughed out of any business deal. He was negotiating with his heart instead of his head, fighting over a dining room set that ended up costing more in legal fees to win than he had paid for it.

"I realized I was acting like a desperate ex-husband instead of a strategic businessman," Steve told me later. "The moment I switched to thinking like a CEO making a business deal, everything changed. We settled in two weeks."

This chapter is about negotiating like the successful man you are, instead of the emotional wreck divorce can reduce you to. Because the moment you start negotiating from a place of desperation, you've already lost.

THE MINDSET THAT CHANGES EVERYTHING

Here's the first rule of successful divorce negotiation: you cannot walk into settlement talks thinking you're going to get everything you want. You just won't. That's not how divorce works. It's not how any negotiation works.

An experienced attorney explained it clearly: "You can't go into a divorce thinking that you're going to get everything you want, that you're keeping everything, or that what you want will determine how everything unfolds. You need to expect that you'll have to make compromises. You may not love those compromises, but if you want this resolved quickly and without costing a fortune, you need to be ready to compromise and accept that you won't get everything you want."

This isn't about being weak or giving up. It's about being realistic so you can be strategic. The men who accept this reality from the beginning end up better off than those who doggedly fight it until they're exhausted and broke.

Think of it this way: in business, you rarely get your opening offer accepted. You start high, they start low, and you work toward a middle ground that both sides can compromise on and live with. Even though the stakes are your children and your financial future, divorce negotiations work the same way.

UNDERSTANDING WHAT JUDGES ACTUALLY CARE ABOUT

Before you make any demands or reject any offers, you must fully understand what would happen if you end up in front of a judge. This gives you leverage in negotiations, because both sides can evaluate offers against what a court would likely order.

Judges care about specific things: the best interests of children above everything else, fair asset division based on state law, each person's ability to pay support, documented facts rather than accusations, and maintaining stability for the kids.

Judges don't care about who cheated, who's the "better" person, your emotional attachment to that damn dining room set, promises that weren't written down, or who "deserves" more.

Understanding these priorities helps you negotiate smarter. If your position aligns with what a judge would likely order, you have strength. If it doesn't, you're negotiating from weakness and need to adjust your expectations accordingly.

THE FIGHT VS. FOLD DECISION FRAMEWORK

For every issue in your divorce, you must decide whether it's worth fighting for. Here's a simple framework to help you choose your battles wisely.

Fight when the issue significantly affects your children's well-being. Say your ex wants to move the kids across the country, or limit your time with them unreasonably, this is worth the battle.

Fight when the financial impact is substantial and long-term. If we're talking about your retirement funds or significant assets, the cost of fighting may be worth it.

Fight when you have strong evidence supporting your position. Don't fight battles you can't win, but if you have clear documentation, you're negotiating from a position of strength.

Fold when the cost of fighting exceeds the value at stake. Don't spend twenty thousand dollars in legal fees to protect a ten-thousand-dollar asset!

Fold when the issue is primarily about pride or revenge. These battles cost more than they're worth and damage your relationship with your kids.

Fold when you have weak evidence or a shaky legal position. Don't throw good money after bad.

Fold when winning would damage your co-parenting relationship. Some victories aren't worth the long-term cost to your children.

THE BUSINESS DEAL APPROACH

Successful businesspeople don't make decisions based on emotion. They're data-driven, weigh their options, and then pick the path that best aligns with their long-term goals. That's exactly how you should approach divorce negotiations.

If this were a business deal, you'd analyze the numbers objectively, consider the opportunity cost of prolonged negotiations, factor in the risk of going to trial, and make decisions based on return on investment, not feelings.

Yet somehow, when it comes to their own divorce, savvy businessmen suddenly start thinking with their hearts instead of their heads. They fight over assets that cost more in legal fees than they're worth. They refuse reasonable offers out of spite. They make decisions that any CEO would recognize as terrible business moves.

Don't be that guy. Approach your divorce like you'd approach any other significant business transaction - clear objectives, realistic expectations, and calculated decisions.

THE COMPROMISE MINDSET

One attorney put it this way: "You can't say 'I have this expectation. I must achieve this goal, or the world's going to end.' That just doesn't work."

Instead, think in ranges and alternatives. Applied to custody, you might ask yourself - what's the minimum time with my children I can accept? What's ideal? What's realistic based on my work schedule and their activities?

For support, what's the maximum I can afford long-term without destroying my ability to rebuild? What's fair based on both of our incomes and expenses? What would a judge likely order?

For assets, what do I actually need to rebuild my life versus what I just want to keep? What has real financial value versus sentimental value? What am I willing to trade to get something more important?

This range thinking gives you flexibility during negotiations. You can make strategic concessions on less important issues to secure what really matters.

AVOIDING THE RECONCILIATION FANTASY

Many men sabotage their negotiations by secretly hoping for

reconciliation, making concessions, thinking it will show their ex they're a good guy worth taking back.

This is normal, but it is dangerous to your negotiation strategy.

If you're negotiating from a place of hoping for reconciliation, you won't protect your interests properly. You'll give away too much, agree to temporary arrangements that become permanent, and avoid making necessary and reasonable demands because you don't want to "rock the boat."

Accept the reality: if you're in divorce negotiations, the marriage is over! Negotiate accordingly. You can be respectful and fair without being naive about the outcome.

THE SETTLEMENT CHECKLIST APPROACH

Approach settlement negotiations like you're working through a business checklist, not fighting for your life. Every issue that needs resolution, no matter how emotionally charged, is just another item to work through methodically.

Start with the easy agreements and build momentum. If you both agree on custody schedules, get that locked down. If you agree on who keeps which car, mark it as complete. The more issues you resolve quickly, the fewer things you have to fight about.

Be specific about everything. Vague agreements lead to future conflicts. If you're splitting retirement accounts, clearly detail how and when. If you're sharing holiday custody, specify which holidays and how transitions will occur.

Consider the long-term consequences. Will this setup work when your kids are teenagers? What if someone loses their job? What if someone wants to move? Address these scenarios now instead of arguing about them later.

Document everything as you go. Don't rely on memory or verbal agreements. If you shake hands on something, get it in writing before moving to the next issue.

THE REALITY CHECK PROCESS

Before you reject any proposal or make any demand, run it through this reality check:

Is this request reasonable, given our financial situation and state law? Will fighting for this cost more than its actual value? Am I asking for this because it's practical... or because I'm angry? If a neutral person heard both sides, would they think this is fair?

If you can't answer these questions objectively, you're probably negotiating from emotion rather than strategy. Step back, get some perspective, and make decisions based on logic, not feelings.

WHAT GOOD ATTORNEYS ACTUALLY DO

They won't tell you what you want to hear. They'll tell you what you need to know. As one attorney explained: "People don't come to me just to hear whatever they want to hear. They're paying me to give them legal advice, to counsel them, and to use my experience with the whole divorce process to help them."

Your attorney should provide you with realistic settlement outcome ranges, explain the costs and benefits of fighting versus compromising, help prioritize issues, and keep you focused on practical concerns rather than emotional ones.

Are they encouraging you to fight every battle or just telling you that you can get everything you want? Yeah, it's time to find a new attorney. Good ones help you make smart decisions, not expensive ones.

MANAGING THE EMOTIONAL TIMELINE

Understanding where you and your spouse are emotionally can help you time your negotiations better. Most divorce cases follow a predictable emotional pattern: fear of the unknown, anger and blame, bargaining and attempts to control outcomes, acceptance of the new reality, and only then — finally — comes resolution and moving forward.

Most people can't negotiate effectively until they at least reach the acceptance phase. If you're still angry or your spouse is still in fear mode, negotiations will be emotionally raw rather than logical.

Sometimes the smartest move is waiting a few weeks or months for emotions to cool down. Pushing for immediate resolution when everyone's still emotional often leads to worse outcomes and higher costs.

THE POWER OF STRATEGIC PATIENCE

One of the most powerful phrases in divorce negotiations is: "Let me think about that and get back to you."

This simple statement buys you time to think or consult with your attorney, prevents emotional decision-making, demonstrates you're calm and intentional, and keeps the negotiation on your terms. While you should ensure that you follow up within 24–48 hours to remain credible and engaged, don't feel pressured to make important decisions on the spot just because someone's waiting for an answer.

Shield Yourself: The Strategic Negotiator's Assessment

Before every negotiation session, remind yourself that you're doing it to resolve practical problems, not for vindication or validation. Your ex-wife isn't your enemy in this process - she's a business partner you're trying to reach agreements with.

Run every decision through the long-term consequences filter: What will this cost or save you over five years? Ten years? How will it affect your relationship with your children? How about your ability to rebuild financially?

Focus on interests rather than positions. Don't just demand what you want — explain why it benefits both sides. If you want more custody time, that's okay, but frame it around what's best for the children, not what you feel you deserve.

Remain flexible about methods but stay firm on core interests. You may not get the exact custody schedule you want, but make sure you protect your ability to maintain a strong relationship with your children.

Before each session, review these questions: What are my actual needs versus wants? What am I willing to trade to get what matters most? What would a reasonable third-party think is fair? How does this compare to what a judge would likely order?

THE LONG-TERM PERSPECTIVE

Remember, you're not just negotiating the end of your marriage - you're negotiating the foundation of your post-divorce life. Every agreement you make now will affect you for years to come.

Think beyond the immediate pain you're in. Focus on what will serve you best in the long run. A settlement that costs less in legal fees, preserves your relationship with your children, and gives you a solid enough foundation to rebuild financially is worth more than any symbolic victory.

The goal isn't to win the divorce - it's to win the next chapter of your life.

ONE MOVE THAT MATTERS

This week, write down your actual settlement goals. Not what would make you happy, but what you actually need to protect your financial future and relationship with your children. These will become your non-negotiables.

Make two lists:

1. "Must Haves" (things you absolutely need)
2. "Would Likes" (things you'd prefer, but could live without)

Share these lists with your attorney and ask for realistic ranges on each item.

Use those ranges to inform your negotiation strategy, rather than trying to get everything you want. Calculated decisions beat emotional, knee-jerk reactions every time.

The men who negotiate from strength rather than desperation get better outcomes and move on with their lives faster. They approach divorce like the successful businessmen they are, not like desperate ex-husbands.

Key Takeaways: Effective negotiation in divorce requires approaching the process like a business transaction rather than an emotional battle. Set realistic expectations, focus on long-term consequences over short-term validation, and remember that settling efficiently serves your interests better than fighting every issue. Men who negotiate from a position of strength rather than desperation tend to achieve better outcomes and move forward more quickly.

CHAPTER 13
DIVORCE-PROOFING YOUR AGREEMENT

A dam thought his divorce was finally over when he signed on the dotted line. The settlement agreement looked professional — twenty-three pages of legalese that his attorney assured him was "standard" — but six months later, a single overlooked word in the college expense clause cost him $18,000 he hadn't budgeted for. His ex-wife's interpretation of "reasonable" college costs included private tutoring, study abroad programs, and graduate school expenses that Adam had never agreed to pay!

Here's how to translate principles into enforceable clauses — so there's no ambiguity when real life shows up.

> "One word can make a big difference in that divorce," Adam told me. "Each attorney is trying to maybe sneak in a word that changes the meaning... you have to understand every written word. And remember, even though it's written there and stated clearly, enforcing it down the road may be another story."

This is why the details matter so much.

Your divorce agreement isn't just a piece of paper that officially ends your marriage. It's the constitution for your post-divorce life. It determines how much money you'll have, how much time you'll spend with your children, and how many future conflicts you'll face.

Nail it, and you'll enjoy peace and clarity for years to come. Get it wrong, and you'll be writing checks to attorneys for problems that could have been prevented.

Just like a marriage starting with two little words, the difference between a good divorce agreement and a nightmare is often just a couple of words. Smart men get those words right the first time.

UNDERSTANDING THE THREE TYPES OF AGREEMENTS

Most people don't realize there are actually three different types of agreements you might encounter during your divorce. Knowing the difference can save you confusion and money.

A **Term Sheet** is basically a bullet-point list of what you've agreed to. Simple and straightforward. For example: "John pays Sally $3,000 per month for nine years."

A **Memorandum of Understanding** has more detail and context. For example: "John pays Sally $3,000 per month spousal support, beginning January 1st, payable by the 1st of each month for 108 months, with payments ending upon Sally's remarriage, cohabitation, or death, whichever occurs first."

A **Final Divorce Agreement** is the comprehensive legal document that covers every possible scenario. This includes the above, plus detailed provisions about what constitutes cohabitation, how payments are made if the 1st falls on a holiday, what happens if John loses his job, modification procedures, enforcement mechanisms, and much more.

The key is making sure you understand which type of document you're signing, as well as what level of detail will be in the final agreement. Don't assume the term sheet will automatically become a detailed final agreement without your input on the specifics.

SMALL WORDS, BIG CONSEQUENCES

I've seen men lose thousands of dollars because they didn't understand the difference between "and" and "or" in their agreements. Small words have huge consequences when they're not chosen carefully.

Vague language like "soon," "promptly," or "in a timely manner" aren't deadlines - they're invitations for conflict. Specific language like "within 30 days of written notice" is clear and enforceable.

Consider communication requirements. "Parents will communicate about the children" is useless. Better language would be: "Parents will communicate via Our Family Wizard app, checking messages at least once every 48 hours. Emergency communications may be made by text message to the following numbers..."

When it comes to decision-making, "Parents will make decisions jointly" sounds cooperative, but is too fluffy... what happens when you disagree? Strategic language would say: "Parents will make educational decisions jointly. If they cannot agree after good faith consultation, Mother has final decision-making authority for educational matters and Father has final decision-making authority for extracurricular activities."

PAUL'S $30,000 LESSON IN VAGUE LANGUAGE

Paul thought his divorce was going smoothly... they used a mediator, agreed on everything quickly, and kept costs low. His mistake was not getting specific enough in the agreement.

The agreement stated, "pickups and drop-offs around 5 PM." His ex interpreted "around" as anywhere from 3 PM to 7 PM, depending on her schedule. It said, "parents will communicate about the children," but didn't specify how, when, or through which method. It mentioned "parties will share extracurricular expenses," but didn't define what counts as extracurricular activities.

Every vague phrase became a battleground of interpretation. Every undefined term became an argument. What started as an "amicable"

$5,000 divorce turned into a three-year, $30,000 nightmare of constant disputes.

"Getting more clarity as to communicating with the kids, really thinking through what that looks like, scheduling, what that looks like, who drops off, who picks up, what times... this piece of paper is like the new rule book. And for someone like me, who wasn't always good at setting boundaries, having third-party objective rules in writing helped a lot," Paul explained.

Paul's story shows how even well-intentioned couples can end up embroiled in expensive conflicts when the language isn't strategic and specific enough.

SPECIAL CONSIDERATIONS FOR HIGH-CONFLICT SITUATIONS

If your ex is high-conflict, your agreement needs airtight, iron-clad protection. No gray areas. No wiggle room. Smart men anticipate problems and seal loopholes before they turn into black holes.

Communication restrictions might mandate all communication be through email or a parenting app, prohibit any phone calls except for actual emergencies, or forbid discussion of adult issues in front of children.

Strict boundaries could mean no unannounced visits or entering each other's homes without permission and clearly defining what constitutes harassment or inappropriate behavior.

Built-in enforcement should include automatic consequences for violations, clear documentation requirements, and streamlined procedures for handling common problems without involving everyone in court each time.

For high-conflict situations, consider including language about therapeutic intervention, parenting coordinators for ongoing disputes, and specific step-by-step protocols for managing disagreements.

GETTING PROFESSIONAL REVIEW, EVEN AFTER MEDIATION

Okay, so let's say you went through mediation and everything feels cooperative. You should still have your own attorney review the final agreement, since they're looking for different things than what the mediator focused on during negotiations.

A review attorney might identify missing protective clauses that could save you money later, tax implications you didn't consider during negotiations, potential enforcement issues that could cost thousands, local law requirements that might have been overlooked, and industry-standard provisions you might be missing.

Questions to ask your review attorney: What's missing that should be included? How would this work in real life, day-to-day? What are the enforcement risks if my ex doesn't comply? Are there any tax surprises I should know about? Is this agreement better or worse than what a judge would likely order?

The cost of attorney review is small compared to the cost of fixing problems later. One client spent $8,000 trying to enforce a poorly written agreement that could have been fixed for $500 during the drafting phase!

THE COLLEGE EXPENSES MINEFIELD

This is a line item that has annihilated many post-divorce budgets. If your agreement mentions college costs, you need precise language that unequivocally states what's covered and what's not. Note that college expenses are not an issue in every jurisdiction, so ensure you know the law where you live.

Basic questions that need clear answers:

What qualifies as "college expenses"? Are we talking just tuition and fees, or also room, board, books, transportation, and spending money? What about graduate school? Study abroad programs? Private tutoring? SAT prep courses?

How much is each parent expected to contribute? A percentage of income? A flat dollar amount? What happens if the child chooses an expensive private school when a state school is available? Who decides which school choice is "reasonable"?

What if your income changes dramatically between now and when your kids reach college age? What if your ex remarries someone wealthy and you're still stuck paying the same percentage? What if the child gets scholarships - do the parents pay less, or does the child get more spending money, drawn from the original sum that remains unchanged?

These questions sound trivial now, but they become costly when your child is eighteen and heading to college!

FUTURE-PROOFING YOUR AGREEMENT

Life changes, and your agreement should be dynamic enough not to require expensive court battles every time it does.

Plan for kids getting older and needing different schedules, job changes that affect income, geographic moves for career opportunities, remarriage or new long-term relationships, changes in childcare needs, and major educational expenses.

Build in modification procedures that start with communication and escalation rather than litigation. For example: "If either parent's income changes by more than 20% for six consecutive months, either parent may request support modification. The process will begin with good faith discussion, proceed to mediation if needed, and only go to court if other methods fail."

Include language about how you'll handle technology changes. Today's communication apps might not exist in five years, so build in flexibility to adopt new tools while maintaining the same communication principles.

SHIELD YOURSELF: THE FINAL REVIEW CHECKLIST

Before you sign any agreement, ask yourself these critical questions:

Do I understand every single provision in plain English? Can I afford these financial obligations in the long-term, not just today? Are my children's interests truly protected in all scenarios? What are the tax implications of these asset divisions and support arrangements? How would each provision be enforced if my ex doesn't comply? Have I had an independent legal review from my own attorney? Am I signing this because it's genuinely good, or because I'm exhausted and want this to be over?

Don't sign if you don't understand major provisions, can't afford the long-term financial commitments, your attorney advises against it, you're being pressured to sign immediately without enough time to review, you haven't had a chance to discuss with your support team, or the terms seem too good to be true.

Take time to read everything, out loud. If you stumble over complex language or can't explain what a provision means in plain English, the language needs to be fixed before you sign.

THE LONG-TERM PERSPECTIVE

Remember, you'll be living with this agreement for years, possibly decades if you have young children. Every holiday schedule, every pickup time, every financial obligation, every decision-making process will be governed by the words in this document.

Spending extra time and money to get the language right will save you significant amounts of both money and conflict down the line. The goal isn't just to end your marriage legally - it's to create a framework that helps both parents move forward successfully, with as little ongoing friction as possible.

Think of your agreement as the foundation of your post-divorce life. A strong foundation supports everything you want to build. A weak foundation leads to problems that grow over time.

ONE MOVE THAT MATTERS

Before signing any agreement, read every word out loud to someone who isn't involved in your divorce - a trusted friend, family member, or advisor. If you can't explain what any sentence means in plain English, the language needs to be clearer.

Have them ask questions about edge cases and unusual situations: What happens if someone gets sick during a scheduled pickup? What if there's a snow day and school is canceled? What if someone is consistently late? What if one parent wants to move? If your agreement doesn't outline clear answers for such predictable problems, you need better language.

Create a simple test: imagine you're explaining each major provision to your teenager. If you can't make it clear to them, it's probably not clear enough for real life.

A good agreement prevents problems with specificity. An excellent agreement solves problems before they happen by anticipating common issues. A strategic agreement does both, all while protecting your future interests and maintaining sufficient flexibility to adapt to life's inevitable changes.

Key Takeaways: The language in your divorce agreement will influence your life after divorce for many years. Every word matters, and each clause must be clear and enforceable because vague language could cost you thousands in future disputes. Take the time and spend the money to get it right the first time, as you might never get another chance to fix serious issues in the language.

CHAPTER 14
MAKING YOUR AGREEMENT WORK LONG-TERM

THE $8,000 LESSON

 "Best money I ever spent," Mark Thompson told me after having his divorce agreement reviewed by a second lawyer. "My buddy, who didn't do that, has spent $8,000 in the past two years just trying to enforce his lousy agreement."

Mark's story highlights a vital truth about divorce agreements: the quality of your agreement shapes your quality of life for years to come. A well-made agreement prevents issues, while a poorly drafted one leads to endless — and costly — problems.

So, the ink is dry on your divorce agreement. You think you're done. Sorry, you're not even close. That carefully crafted document you just signed isn't just a piece of paper that ends your marriage — it's the blueprint for your post-divorce life. It determines how much money you'll have, how much time you'll spend with your children, and how many future conflicts you'll face.

This chapter is about the reality of living with your agreement, not just having one.

UNDERSTANDING THE ENFORCEMENT REALITY

Even a perfect agreement is only as good as your ability to enforce it when violations occur. Understanding enforcement realities helps you design better agreements and respond strategically when problems arise.

The Hard Truth About Enforcement: As one father learned, "As much blood, sweat, and tears as you might have already put into that document, make it as thorough as possible. But keep in mind that enforcing what's written there could be very expensive." This doesn't mean you should accept a weak agreement because enforcement is difficult. It means you should design your agreement strategically to make following it easier than breaking it.

Enforcement Mechanisms Vary by State: Different states have different tools for enforcing divorce agreements, and understanding your options helps you build stronger agreements and respond effectively to violations.

Contempt of court proceedings are available in all states when someone willfully violates court orders. However, the burden of proof varies significantly. Some states require "clear and convincing evidence," while others use "preponderance of evidence" standards. The consequences also differ — some states favor monetary sanctions, while others may impose jail time for repeated violations.

Wage garnishment for support is available nationwide, but with different procedures and limitations. Federal law allows garnishment, but only up to a certain percentage of your income. Some states have additional protections or simplified procedures.

Asset Seizure and Property Liens vary significantly by state. Community property states (Arizona, California, Idaho, Louisiana, Nevada, New Mexico, Texas, Washington, and Wisconsin) have different enforcement mechanisms than equitable distribution states. Some states allow immediate liens on property for unpaid support, while others require additional court proceedings.

Professional license suspension is available in most states for unpaid child support, but it varies for other violations. Some states can suspend driver's licenses, professional licenses, and even hunting and fishing licenses for non-payment of support obligations.

IMPORTANT STATE VARIATIONS TO DISCUSS WITH YOUR ATTORNEY:

- There may be a statute of limitations for enforcement actions
- Requirements for contempt proceedings (some states require specific language in original orders)
- Available remedies for different types of violations
- Procedures for cross-state enforcement when parties live in different states
- Interest rates and collection fees that can be added to unpaid obligations

Strategic Agreement Design: Smart agreements are easier to follow than to break. Incorporate natural consequences that do not require court intervention. Include escalation procedures that give people opportunities to resolve issues before they escalate into costly court battles.

For example, instead of going directly to court when someone breaks the parenting schedule, your agreement might require written notice of the violation, 48 hours to respond and fix the issue, mediation if violations persist, and court action only as a last resort.

Document everything. Require written notice for all changes. Implement automatic triggers for common situations. Make violations clear and easy to demonstrate.

UNDERSTANDING LEGAL MODIFICATION STANDARDS

Life changes, and your agreement needs to anticipate this reality while meeting legal standards for modifications. Understanding these requirements helps you build better original agreements and know when modifications are possible.

Support Modification Standards: Courts require a "substantial change in circumstances" for support modifications, but this definition varies significantly by jurisdiction. Generally, it means the change must be substantial (think like a 10–15% income change or more), continuing (not temporary), and involuntary (not chosen by the paying party).

Custody Modification Standards: Courts typically require either a "material change in circumstances" that impacts the child's best interests, or evidence that the current arrangement is harmful to the child. Some states also have specific waiting periods (typically 1–2 years) before modifications can be sought, unless emergency circumstances exist.

Correct Legal Framework for Modifications in your Agreement:

For Support Modifications: "Either party may petition for modification of support obligations upon showing a substantial, continuing, and involuntary change in circumstances that makes the current order unreasonable. Substantial change means an increase or decrease of at least 15% in the paying party's gross income lasting longer than three consecutive months."

For Custody Modifications: "The court may modify custody arrangements upon a showing that: (1) circumstances have materially changed since the original order affecting the child's best interests, and (2) modification would serve the child's best interests. No modification may be sought within 12 months of the original order except in cases involving risk of harm to the child."

Key State Variations in Modification Standards:

- **Income Changes:** Each state has a definition of "sufficient change in income"
- **Time Requirements:** Waiting periods range from 6 months to 2 years for custody modifications
- **Burden of Proof:** Some states require "clear and convincing evidence" while others use "preponderance of evidence"
- **Cost of Living Adjustments:** Some states allow automatic adjustments, others require separate petitions

The key is to ensure you take modification applications out of the court's control. Be sure you clearly specify what triggers a modification and how it will be determined.

BUILDING FUTURE-PROOF PROVISIONS

Strategic agreements anticipate common life changes and provide mechanisms to handle them without expensive court battles.

Predictable Life Changes to Address:

Children's Changing Needs: As children grow older, they require different schedules, have school and activity commitments, and develop personal preferences regarding parenting time. Good agreements include age-appropriate adjustments and procedures for considering children's input as they mature.

Career and Income Changes: Job changes, promotions, career transitions, and economic downturns are expected during the course of a long-term agreement. Therefore, include procedures for handling temporary income variations, career transition periods, and automatic review triggers.

Geographic Relocation: Career opportunities, family needs, or remarriage may require one parent to move. Cover the notification requirements for such a move, its effect on parenting schedules, transportation responsibilities, and modification procedures.

Educational Expenses: College costs, private school choices, tutoring needs, and special educational requirements often emerge years after divorce. Clarify contribution formulas, decision-making procedures, and limits on responsibilities.

Healthcare and Insurance Changes: Job changes impact insurance coverage, children's medical needs evolve, and healthcare costs rise over time. Include procedures for coverage decisions, cost sharing, and provider changes.

Future-Proofing Language Examples:

For Income Changes: "If either party experiences an involuntary income change exceeding 20% for more than 90 days, they may request support review through the following process: (1) 30 days written notice with income documentation, (2) good faith negotiation for 30 days, (3) mediation if the parties cannot reach an agreement, and finally (4) court petition only after completing steps 1–3."

For Relocation: "Any proposed relocation of more than 50 miles from the current residence requiring modification of parenting schedules must include: (1) 90 days advance written notice, (2) detailed relocation plan including proposed schedule modifications, (3) 60-day good faith negotiation period, (4) best interests analysis by the court if agreement cannot be reached."

For College Expenses: "Parents will contribute to reasonable college expenses based on their proportional incomes at the time expenses are incurred, with total contributions not to exceed the cost of in-state tuition at [State University]. Decisions about college selection and expense allocation will be made jointly, with mediation for disputes prior to involving the court."

ENFORCEMENT STRATEGY AND DOCUMENTATION

Having a strategic response plan when violations happen saves money and boosts effectiveness.

Documentation Requirements: Keep comprehensive records of all violations, including dates, times, witnesses, and impacts. Save all communications regarding the violations. Take photographs as evidence when applicable. Maintain a violation log that identifies patterns over time, not just isolated incidents.

Communication About Violations: Always address violations in writing first. Be specific about which provision was violated and what remedy you're seeking. Set reasonable deadlines for compliance. Remain professional and factual, avoiding emotional language that could undermine your position.

Escalation Procedures: Follow any escalation steps specified in your agreement. If none are outlined, start with direct communication, then attempt mediation if available, before filing court motions. Record each step to demonstrate you acted in good faith to resolve the issue.

Strategic Considerations: Choose your battles carefully. Not every violation warrants enforcement action. Consider the cost versus benefit of enforcement, the pattern of violations versus isolated incidents, and the impact on your children and co-parenting relationship.

WHEN AGREEMENTS NEED UPDATES

Even well-crafted agreements sometimes need updates as life circumstances change substantially.

Signs Your Agreement Needs Updating:

- Constant disputes over the interpretation of existing language
- Changed circumstances make compliance difficult or impossible
- Children's needs or preferences that differ significantly from current arrangements
- Financial changes that make current obligations unreasonable
- One party repeatedly violates the terms due to changed circumstances

Before rushing to court: Try structured renegotiation. Propose specific changes in writing, explaining why they're necessary and how they benefit everyone. Consider mediation to resolve issues cooperatively. Document all attempts at resolution to demonstrate to courts that you tried to work it out.

Legal Standards for Modifications: Courts are more likely to modify agreements when you can show you tried to work it out first, the current agreement isn't serving the children's best interests, and you have a specific, reasonable proposal for improvement based on changed circumstances.

THE INVESTMENT IN QUALITY

Getting your agreement right might cost more upfront — attorney review, multiple drafts, detailed negotiations — but strategic people understand this is an investment, not an expense.

The Long-Term Perspective: You get one chance to create the framework that will govern your post-divorce life. Once it's signed and filed with the court, making changes is difficult and expensive. Don't rush this part just because you're tired of the process. Don't accept vague language because someone says, "It's fine." Don't skip professional review to save a few hundred dollars.

Professional Review Benefits: A qualified family law attorney reviewing your final agreement can identify missing protective clauses, recognize tax implications you may have overlooked, detect enforcement issues early, ensure compliance with local law requirements, and verify that industry-standard provisions are included.

Questions for Your Review Attorney:

- What's missing that should be included in this agreement?
- How would these provisions work in real-world situations?
- What are the enforcement risks of the current language?
- Are there any tax implications we haven't considered?
- Is this agreement better or worse than what a judge would likely order?

LIVING WITH REALITY

At the end of the day, no agreement is perfect. No matter how detailed, something unexpected will arise... your ex will interpret something differently than you intended, and life will inevitably present situations your agreement doesn't explicitly address.

The 90% Rule: Establish an agreement that covers 90% of situations clearly, with reasonable mechanisms to handle the remaining 10% without court intervention. While perfect precision isn't achievable, clear guidelines and good faith procedures can resolve most issues.

Strategic Flexibility: Choose your battles wisely. Not every violation calls for enforcement. Not every disagreement requires legal resolution. Sometimes, being right costs more than winning.

One father explained his approach: "I could spend $5,000 fighting about holiday schedules, or I could just be flexible and spend that money on a vacation with my kids. Easy choice, when you think about it strategically."

SHIELD YOURSELF: THE AGREEMENT MANAGEMENT SYSTEM

Create a systematic approach for managing your agreement long-term:

Agreement Operations Manual: Document key dates and deadlines, payment schedules and amounts, holiday rotation schedules, communication protocols, and modification procedures. Having this quick reference prevents mistakes and helps you spot violations early.

Regular Review Schedule: Every six months, assess whether the agreement is working as intended, any conflicts that keep arising, what changes in circumstances have occurred, and what modifications might be needed. Keep a simple log of issues — not to build a case, but to identify patterns that might need addressing.

Professional Relationships: Maintain relationships with the professionals who helped create your agreement. They understand your situation and can provide guidance when issues arise. This includes your attorney, mediator, financial advisor, and therapist.

Documentation Habits: Continue documenting significant interactions, decisions, and changes even after your divorce is final. Good documentation protects you from future disputes and provides evidence if modifications become necessary.

Communication Standards: Maintain professional communication standards, even — and especially — when frustrated. All communications could become evidence in future proceedings, so stay factual, brief, and focused on finding solutions rather than placing blame.

ONE MOVE THAT MATTERS

This week, create your Agreement Operations Manual. Write down all key dates and deadlines from your agreement, payment schedules and amounts, holiday rotation schedules, communication protocols, and modification procedures.

Share relevant parts with your support team so they can help you stay compliant and protected. Having this quick reference prevents costly mistakes and helps you implement your agreement successfully.

Remember: your agreement is the foundation, but how you implement and live with it determines how sturdy your quality of life is post-divorce.

Key Takeaways: To ensure your agreement lasts in the long term, you must make informed decisions about enforcement, modification, and practical application. The best agreement in the world is useless if you can't enforce it affordably or modify it when life changes. Design for the reality of post-divorce life, with precise enforcement mechanisms, reasonable modification procedures, and future-proofing provisions that anticipate predictable changes.

PART FIVE
THE PHOENIX PHASE

CHAPTER 15
SURVIVING THE FIRST YEAR

THE DIVORCE HANGOVER

 "It's like you have a divorce hangover."

That's how Sarah described the year after her divorce was finalized. After having spent so much time and energy fighting through the process, when it was over, she didn't know what to do with herself!

I didn't realize the significance at first, until later, when everyone kept telling me that the first year after your divorce is going to be the hardest. It's harder in some ways than actually getting divorced. And I was like, what are you talking about? I am so happy. I'm free. Oh my God. I totally didn't get it. But then, when I had some distance, I realized what they were talking about.

If you're reading this chapter, congratulations. You made it through the war. Your divorce is final. The legal battles are over. Now comes the part nobody really prepares you for — figuring out how to survive your new life.

The first year after divorce is brutal, but it's also the foundation for everything that comes next. Strategic men prepare for it instead of getting blindsided by it.

UNDERSTANDING THE PSYCHOLOGICAL RECOVERY FRAMEWORK

Divorce recovery follows predictable psychological patterns. Understanding these patterns helps you navigate them strategically rather than feeling like you're losing your mind.

The Grief Cycle in Divorce Recovery: Even if it was your choice, you will still grieve the loss of your envisioned future, your intact family, your financial stability, and your sense of identity as a married person. Grief doesn't follow a straight path — it's experienced in waves, often catching you off guard.

Identity Reconstruction Process: Your post-divorce identity development progresses through three clear stages: disintegration (who am I now?), exploration (trying out new versions of yourself), and integration (adapting to your new identity). Most men tend to skip the middle stage — jumping from confusion directly to certainty — but this usually leads to setbacks.

Attachment System Recalibration: Your nervous system has spent years adjusting to being part of a couple. Now, it needs to readjust to being single again. This physical shift can cause various symptoms like anxiety, insomnia, digestive problems, and mood swings that aren't related to your emotional state!

Understanding these patterns helps you respond strategically: When you feel like you're going crazy, you're probably just going through normal recovery phases. When you feel stuck, you might be resisting a necessary part of the process. When you feel overwhelmed, your system may just need more time to adjust.

THE EMOTIONAL TIMELINE NOBODY TALKS ABOUT

It can be an emotional roller coaster. One day, you feel like you can conquer the world. Next, you can barely get out of bed. Let me walk you through what's normal in early post-divorce life so you don't think you're losing your mind.

The Relief Phase (Months 1–3)

You might feel relief. The conflict is over. The uncertainty is over. You can finally breathe and start planning your life. You sleep better. You feel optimistic. This is normal and healthy.

What's Really Happening: Your nervous system is recovering from all that chronic stress. You're experiencing the psychological equivalent of finally being able to rest after running a marathon. Your body and mind are getting much-needed recovery after the crisis.

Strategic Response: Avoid making any major life decisions during this phase. Don't buy a sports car, move across the country, and definitely don't propose to the first woman who smiles at you! The relief is real, but it's not the full picture of your emotional landscape.

Common Mistakes: Many men interpret this relief as "being over it" and resist the harder emotional work that comes next. They jump into dating, make big purchases, or take risks they'll regret when reality sets in.

The Reality Phase (Months 3–6)

Reality hits. The loneliness sets in. The financial stress becomes real. Co-parenting turns out to be harder than you thought. Your social life needs a complete rebuild. You realize this isn't temporary — this is your new life.

What's Really Happening: The adrenaline has long worn off, and your brain is now processing the full scope of changes in your life. This is when the real grief work begins, and it's often more intense than what you experienced during the actual divorce process.

Strategic Response: This is when a lot of guys get stuck. They get depressed. They isolate. They make poor decisions because they're overwhelmed. Don't be that guy. Calculated decisions beat emotional drift every time.

Essential Support Strategies: This is when therapy becomes more valuable, not less. Your support system needs to be most active during this phase. Physical exercise becomes critical for managing anxiety and depression. Maintaining routines provides stability when emotions are chaotic.

The Adjustment Phase (Months 6–12)

You start figuring it out. You develop new routines. You make new friends. You get better at handling the kids' schedules and your ex's attitude. Some days are good, some suck, but gradually the good outnumber the bad.

What's Really Happening: Your identity is beginning to solidify around your new circumstances. You're developing competence in areas you felt lost before. Your nervous system is adapting to your new normal.

Strategic Response: This is when you can start making more significant life changes, but you must remain cautious about making major decisions, such as remarriage, career changes, or relocating. Focus on building systems and habits that support long-term stability.

Key Milestones: You can think about your ex without your day being ruined. You can enjoy time alone without feeling desperate for company. You can make decisions based on what you want, not just reacting to circumstances.

IDENTITY REBUILDING STRATEGIES

One of the most challenging aspects of post-divorce life is figuring out who you are when you're not part of a couple. This identity work is essential, but often overlooked.

Reclaiming Your Pre-Marriage Self

Reconnecting with Old Interests: What did you enjoy before you got married? Anything that got lost in the relationship? Music, sports, hobbies, friendships, travel, activities? Part of recovery involves reconnecting with aspects of yourself that have become dormant during marriage.

Reviving Dormant Dreams: What goals or ambitions did you shelve "for the family"? This doesn't mean abandoning responsibility to them, but it might mean revisiting career aspirations, creative pursuits, or personal goals that were put on hold.

Rebuilding Old Friendships: Marriage often shifts social circles toward couple friends. After a divorce, you may need to reconnect with individual friends who can understand and support you through relationship changes. Reach out to old friends who knew you before you got married.

Developing Your New Identity

Exploring New Aspects of Yourself: Divorce often reveals strengths you didn't know you had and preferences you never explored. Maybe you discover you're more social than you thought, or that you actually enjoy solitude more than you realized!

Developing New Competencies: Many married couples specialize — one handles finances, the other handles social planning, and so on. Post-divorce, you will likely need to develop competencies to get up to speed in areas your spouse previously handled. This can be empowering once you get past the initial learning curve.

Creating New Narratives: How do you tell your story now? Not just the divorce story, but your life story. What are you moving toward, not just what are you moving away from? Developing a forward-looking narrative can aid in dating, career decisions, and personal motivation.

Integration Strategies

Values Clarification: What really matters to you now? Divorce often clarifies the values that became muddled during an unhappy marriage. Use this clarity to make decisions about how to spend your time, money, and energy.

Boundary Setting: A part of having a healthy identity involves knowing what you will and won't accept in relationships, work, and life in general. Divorce often teaches these lessons the hard way, but the resulting knowledge is still valuable for all future decisions.

Purpose Development: Beyond just surviving divorce, what do you want your life to be about? This might involve career changes, community involvement, creative pursuits, or relationship goals that align with your authentic self.

BUILDING YOUR RECOVERY SUPPORT SYSTEM

You need various types of support during your first year, and each serves a different purpose.

Professional Support Network

Therapist for Emotional Processing: Choose someone who specializes in men's issues and divorce recovery, not just any therapist who is available or the only one covered by insurance in your area. You need a therapist who understands the unique challenges men face after divorce and can help you process emotions effectively instead of just venting.

Financial Advisor for Future Planning: Your financial life has changed dramatically. You need professional help rebuilding wealth, planning for retirement with new parameters, and making smart decisions about major purchases and investments.

Attorney for Ongoing Issues: Even after a divorce is final, problems can still occur. Working with an attorney who is familiar with your case helps prevent costly mistakes when issues arise.

Career Coach if Needed: If divorce is spurring career changes, professional guidance can help you navigate transitions strategically rather than making decisions based purely on emotion or financial desperation.

Peer Support Network

Other Divorced Fathers: Nobody understands your situation like other men who've been through it. Both formal support groups, like the Men's Divorce Network, and informal friendships with men who have successfully navigated post-divorce life will give you invaluable practical advice and hope.

Men's Groups: Whether focused on divorce recovery, personal development, or just friendship, men's groups provide accountability and perspective that's hard to get elsewhere. Many men discover they prefer male friendships to the couple of friends they had during marriage. Again, consider mensdivorcenetwork.com.

Professional Networking: Your career might require extra focus after divorce. Building professional relationships offers both career prospects and social links with people who share your work interests.

Family and Friend Support

Family members who knew you before marriage—such as parents, siblings, and extended family—can help you reconnect with your core identity when you feel lost or untethered.

Individual Friends: Friends who can stay connected with you regardless of your relationship status are invaluable. These may include old friends from before marriage or new friends who relate to you as an individual.

Your Children's Extended Network: Teachers, coaches, and other parents can provide both practical support and social connections. Being involved in your children's activities keeps you connected to the community.

Spiritual and Community Support

Meaning-Making Resources: Whether organized religion, philosophy, meditation, or nature-based spirituality, having something that connects you to meaning beyond your immediate circumstances helps foster perspective and resilience.

Community Involvement: Participating in volunteering, community organizations, or local groups provides social connection and helps contribute to something bigger than yourself.

This can be especially valuable when you're feeling isolated or sorry for yourself.

Physical Community: Your neighborhood, gym, regular activities, or local establishments where you're recognized and welcomed can provide stability and consistent social interaction.

COMMON SETBACKS AND STRATEGIC SOLUTIONS

Recovery isn't linear and knowing what setbacks to expect helps you handle them strategically rather than feeling like you're failing.

Emotional Setbacks

Anniversary Reactions: Significant dates during your marriage, such as your wedding anniversary, birthdays, and holidays, can trigger unexpected grief even when you think you're "over it." This is normal and usually temporary.

Strategic Response: Prepare in advance for challenging dates. Keep support people ready. Build new positive connections with these dates. Expect emotional reactions — anticipate them, and have a plan.

Loneliness Waves: Even when you're enjoying independence, waves of loneliness can hit unexpectedly, especially during times when you would have shared experiences with your spouse.

Strategic Response: Create a network of people you can reach out to when loneliness hits. Develop solo activities you genuinely enjoy. Remember that loneliness is different from being alone — you can feel lonely in a crowd and content when you're by yourself.

Dating Disappointments: Woah there... go easy on yourself. Take it slow. When you start dating again, disappointments might bring up grief over your marriage and fears about your future. Bad dates can leave you feeling hopeless about finding love again.

Strategic Response: Don't start dating until you're emotionally stable. See dating as a way to build skills, not as a guarantee of a specific result. Set realistic expectations. Don't pressure early relationships to be "the one." And remember, it's okay to just have fun!

Practical Setbacks

Financial Stress: Unexpected expenses, income changes, or financial mistakes can lead to stress that impacts your emotional stability and decision-making abilities.

Strategic Response: Build emergency funds quickly. Seek professional financial advice early. Make conservative financial choices during your first year. Don't use money to fix emotional issues.

Co-Parenting Conflicts: Disagreements with your ex about children can trigger old patterns and create stress that overshadows your entire life.

Strategic Response: Maintain a professional and child-centered tone in communication. Avoid emotional triggers. Record all interactions. Seek professional assistance (such as parenting coordinator or family therapist) if problematic patterns emerge.

Health Issues: Stress, lifestyle changes, and emotional upheaval can affect physical health. Health problems can then create additional stress and depression.

Strategic Response: Prioritize basic health habits, even when you don't feel like it. Get regular medical checkups. Exercise for stress management, not just fitness. Don't self-medicate with alcohol, food, or substances.

Social Setbacks

Friend Loss: Some friends will choose sides or feel uncomfortable with your divorce. The resulting social isolation can increase depression and poor decision-making.

Strategic Response: Accept that some friendships won't stick around. Focus on building relationships that do. Invest in individual friendships rather than just a couple of friends. Be proactive about social connections rather than waiting for others to reach out.

Family Complications: Extended family relationships may change, especially if they're confused about loyalty or feel caught in the middle.

Strategic Response: Communicate directly with family members about your needs and boundaries. Avoid putting your family in the middle of conflicts with your ex. Focus on relationships with people who can support you appropriately.

Identity Confusion: There may come a time when you feel like you no longer know who you are or what you want from life.

Strategic Response: This is normal and usually temporary. Turn to professional help to sort through identity questions. Try new things without committing permanently. Give yourself time to rediscover interests and preferences.

THE YEAR OF FIRSTS

"The year of firsts" means the first year of holidays, birthdays, anniversaries, and major events you experience as a divorced man. Each "first" is a choice point. What do you want to keep from your old life? What needs to change? What new traditions do you want to create?

Methodical approach to Firsts: Don't just survive these moments — use them to build something better. Each first gives you an opportunity to consciously choose how you want to handle similar situations going forward.

The First Holiday Without Your Kids

There's no way around it… this one hits every divorced father hard. I remember my first Thanksgiving without my daughter. The hardest thing, I think, in a divorce situation is splitting the holidays and not having your kids with you during those major or important holidays.

Strategic Response: Do something meaningful for yourself. Don't just sit alone or with your old pal Jack Daniels, feeling sorry for yourself. Visit family, volunteer somewhere, travel, or create a new tradition with other divorced friends. Establish new celebrations with your kids on your days. Maybe you celebrate Christmas on December 26th or Thanksgiving the Friday after. Kids adapt to new traditions better than adults do. Focus on making your time with them special rather than mourning the time you don't have. Quality beats quantity when you're intentional about it.

First Social Events as a Single Man

Going to weddings, parties, or professional events alone can feel awkward and highlight your changed status. You may feel like people are judging you or feeling sorry for you.

Strategic Response: Begin with events where you know people well and feel comfortable. Practice introducing yourself as a single person until it becomes natural. Focus on enjoying the event itself, rather than your relationship status. Bring a friend if it feels appropriate, but avoid relying on this as a long-term solution.

First Major Decisions as a Single Person

From choosing where to live to planning vacations and managing your children's needs, making decisions alone after years of joint decision-making can feel overwhelming or freeing, depending on the day.

Strategic Response: Start with smaller decisions to build confidence. Use your support network for advice but make the final decisions yourself. Document what works so you can repeat successful decision-making processes.

BUILDING BASIC STABILITY

The first year is about survival and stabilization. You're not trying to thrive yet — you're trying to establish routines, handle logistics, and process the emotional upheaval without falling apart. Think of it as building a foundation. You can't build a skyscraper on quicksand. The first year is about digging down, mixing up a whole bunch of crap, then letting it set to create solid ground for everything that comes next.

Establishing New Routines

Morning Routines: How you start your day impacts everything that comes afterward. Create a morning routine that includes physical activity, quiet time for planning or reflection, and an activity that brings you joy or satisfaction.

Evening Routines: How you end your day influences your sleep quality and emotional well-being. Create an evening routine that helps you reflect on the day and get ready for sleep.

Weekly Routines: Having predictable weekly activities offers structure and something to anticipate. This could include exercise classes, social events, children's activities, or personal time.

Monthly Routines: Larger planning and review activities help you stay on track with bigger goals. Monthly financial reviews, social planning, and personal assessment help prevent drift.

Creating Your Physical Environment

Your Living Space: Make your home truly yours. This doesn't require costly renovations but should reflect your style and enhance your well-being. Clean, organized spaces promote emotional stability.

Work Environment: If possible, make changes to your work environment that support your new life. This may involve updating your schedule, adjusting your workspace, or revising your professional relationships.

Social Environments: Identify places where you feel comfortable and welcome as a single person. These might be gyms, community centers, places of worship, or local establishments.

MASTERING CO-PARENTING BASICS

Co-parenting is one of the biggest challenges of the first year, since you're dealing with your own emotional chaos while also trying to provide stability for your children.

The Foundation Principle: Put your children first in every decision. Not what's most convenient for you, not what pisses off your ex the least, but what's genuinely best for your kids.

Communication Strategy: Communicate like business partners — professional, factual, child-focused — saving the personal stuff for your therapist or friends. Use email or co-parenting apps to create records and reduce emotional reactivity.

Consistency Approach: Kids need stability. Try to keep similar rules and expectations in both homes whenever possible. Don't undermine the other parent on things like bedtime or diet just because you can. Work together on major decisions affecting your children.

Conflict Management: Don't compete to be the "fun parent" or the "better parent." Focus on being good co-parents. Avoid involving children in adult conflicts. Resolve disputes away from children.

Time and Patience: Your co-parenting relationship will evolve. What doesn't work now might work better in six months. Be patient with the process and with each other. Focus on long-term patterns rather than individual incidents.

SUCCESS MARKERS FOR YEAR ONE

How do you know if you're on track? Here are the markers of a successful first year:

Child Indicators: Your kids are stable and adjusting well to the new routine. They feel secure in their relationships with both parents. They're not showing signs of emotional distress or behavioral problems related to the divorce.

Relationship Indicators: You can have a business conversation with your ex without it ruining your day. You can be in the same room without major conflict. You've established functional communication patterns.

Personal Health Indicators: You're sleeping better, have more energy than during the divorce process, and are not using substances to cope with emotions. You're maintaining basic self-care and health habits.

Social Indicators: You've developed at least one new friendship or strengthened an old one. You have people you can call when you need support. You're not completely isolated or only socializing with work colleagues.

Stability Indicators: You have a regular routine that provides structure to your life. You can handle unexpected challenges without falling apart. You've made progress on at least one area of self-improvement — fitness, career, finances, or personal growth.

Future Orientation: You're seeing the light at the end of the tunnel and envisioning a positive future for yourself and your children. You have goals and plans that go beyond just surviving. You feel hopeful more often than hopeless.

You're not perfect, but you're functional. You're not thriving yet, but you're not just surviving anymore either.

SHIELD YOURSELF: THE FIRST YEAR SURVIVAL KIT

Create your emotional survival kit for tough days:

Support Contact List: A list of trusted people you can call when you're struggling, including their preferred contact methods and times when they're typically available.

Mood Improvement Activities: A list of activities that reliably improve your mood — exercise, music, hobbies, nature, creative activities, social activities, or spiritual practices.

Goal and Purpose Reminders: Written reminders of your goals and why you're working toward them, including photos, quotes, or other visual reminders that reconnect you with your motivation.

Communication Tools: Emergency phrases for difficult conversations with your ex, templates for common communication needs, and reminders about staying professional and child-focused.

Crisis Management Plan: A plan for handling holidays, birthdays, and other emotional triggers, including alternative activities, support people, and coping strategies.

Professional Resources: Contact details for your therapist, attorney, financial advisor, and other support professionals, including emergency contacts outside of regular hours when applicable.

Keep this kit accessible. You'll need it on hard days and having it ready to roll prevents you from making poor decisions when your emotional resources are depleted.

ONE MOVE THAT MATTERS

This week, identify one area of your first-year survival that needs attention — emotional support, physical health, financial stability, co-parenting, or social connection — and make one specific commitment to improve that area, with a concrete deadline for completion.

If it's emotional support, look up therapists who focus on men's divorce recovery and book an appointment. If it's physical health, plan three workouts for this week and prepare your meals ahead of time. If financial stability is a concern, create a simple budget and emergency fund plan by Sunday. If it's co-parenting, set up one new communication rule with your ex and talk about it with your children, if they're old enough. If it's social connection, reach out to one friend to make plans and find one new social activity to try.

Small actions build momentum. Momentum creates stability. Stability lays the foundation for everything that comes next.

Sorry, the first year is about survival — not success. It's about building a solid foundation, not achieving greatness. But if you approach this year strategically, you'll be on solid footing for the transformation that comes next.

Key Takeaways: The first year after divorce is primarily about psychological recovery, rebuilding identity, and establishing a foundation, rather than undergoing a transformation. Your goal is to understand normal recovery patterns, establish a basic level of stability in all areas of your life, and build the support systems necessary for long-term success. Handle this year strategically, with sufficient professional support and realistic expectations, and you'll have a solid foundation for rebuilding and thriving in year two and beyond.

CHAPTER 16
STABILIZING YOUR NEW LIFE

Marcus sat in his apartment one Tuesday morning, drinking coffee and looking at his calendar. For the first time in two years, he realized he wasn't stressed about what the day would bring. His kids were doing well in school. His ex-wife had actually texted "thank you" last week when he handled a school pickup she'd forgotten about. His bank account was growing instead of shrinking. Most importantly, he could look in the mirror and recognize himself again.

 "I'm not just surviving anymore," Marcus told his divorce coach during their monthly check-in. "I think I'm actually building something here."

Congratulations! You've made it through the worst part. The first year of divorce is behind you. You're not waking up in panic mode anymore. The kids have settled into the routine. You can have a normal conversation with your ex without it ruining your whole day. You're sleeping through the night again.

Now comes a different challenge. You're no longer in crisis, but you're not thriving yet either. You're in what some experts call the "stabilization phase" - the critical period in which you either build a strong foundation for your future, or drift into mediocrity.

This chapter is about taking the right steps to go from just getting by to actively building something solid. You're ready to become the man you want to be, not just the man who survived his divorce.

REBUILDING SELF-TRUST AFTER THE STORM

One of the toughest parts of life after divorce is learning to trust yourself again. After having made what feels like the biggest mistake of your life — marrying the wrong person — how are you possibly supposed to trust your judgment about anything? The answer starts with small wins and consistent action. You rebuild self-trust the same way you build physical strength - one rep at a time.

Start with your morning routine. Get up at the same time every day. Make your bed. Exercise, even if it's just ten pushups. Eat a decent breakfast. These small acts of self-discipline, right off the bat like that, will do wonders when it comes to rebuilding confidence in your ability to follow through.

One recently divorced father put it this way: "I started with just making my bed every morning. Sounds stupid, but after months of chaos, having one thing I could control completely made a difference. Then I added working out three times a week. Then cooking real meals. Each thing I did built on the last one."

Self-trust grows when you do what you say you're going to do, especially when itis something for yourself. Make small commitments, keep them, and your confidence will follow your actions.

BUILDING YOUR FINANCIAL FOUNDATION

Financial stability is the bedrock of everything else you want to build. You can't be the father you want to be or the man you want to become if you're constantly stressed about money. If you haven't already, create a simple budget that reflects your new situation. Include child support, alimony, and all the new costs of managing two households. Be honest about your spending on eating out, entertainment, and emotional expenses.

Next, automate your savings. Even if it's just fifty dollars a week, set up an automatic transfer to a separate account. You need to rebuild your emergency fund from scratch. Most financial experts recommend three to six months of expenses. Perhaps that seems insurmountable right now, so start with whatever you can manage.

Consider this your "never again" fund. It's insurance against ever being trapped in a bad situation because you can't afford to leave. One divorced man explained it perfectly: "I never want to stay somewhere I don't want to be just because I can't afford to go."

If your income took a hit during the divorce, look at ways to increase it. This might involve asking for a raise, taking on freelance work, or developing a new skill that enhances your value. Don't accept this lower standard of living as permanent!

GETTING YOUR BODY BACK

Physical fitness after divorce isn't about vanity — though looking better doesn't hurt — it's about reclaiming your energy, confidence, and mental health.

Many men gain weight during divorce because of stress eating, drinking too much, or just neglecting themselves. Others lose weight due to not eating enough or excessive stress. Either way, your body probably needs attention.

Start simple. Find a form of exercise you can do consistently, not something you'll do once and quit. This might be walking, lifting weights, playing basketball, swimming, or martial arts. The key is consistency over intensity.

Exercise becomes especially important when you're dealing with depression or anxiety. Physical activity is among the most effective treatments for both conditions. It's free, has no negative side effects, and helps you become stronger at the same time. As an added benefit, make it social if possible. Join a gym, find a workout partner, or play in a recreational league. The resulting social connections are as valuable as the physical benefits.

CREATING BETTER RELATIONSHIPS

Your divorce taught you some hard lessons about relationships. Now you get to apply what you learned the hard way to build better connections with everyone in your life.

Start with your children. If you have kids, these relationships are your most important project. You have a chance to be more present and intentional as a father than you were as a married man. Take advantage of it. Create special traditions with your kids that are just yours. Maybe it's Saturday morning pancakes, throwing a baseball in the park, or teaching them to cook. These moments build the foundation of your relationship for the rest of your life.

Build new friendships, too. Many men realize after divorce that their social life was entirely managed by their ex-wife. Now you get to choose your own friends based on shared interests and values, not just couple compatibility!

Join groups where you'll meet like-minded men. This could be a cycling club, a volunteer organization, a professional group, or a men's support group. The goal is to build relationships through shared activities and interests.

Don't overlook professional relationships either. Your network is more important now, especially if you're thinking about career changes. Spend time on connections that can open doors, create opportunities, or offer advice.

IMPROVING CO-PARENTING COMMUNICATION

Look, you don't have to be friends with your ex-wife, but you do need to be effective co-parents. The better this relationship works, the better everything else in your life works.

Keep all communication professional. Be factual, child-focused, and business-like. Save personal conversations for others. You're no longer her husband, so you're not responsible for her feelings or issues.

Set clear boundaries early on. Offer help when appropriate, but avoid falling back into old habits. If she calls crying about her car breaking down, you can give her the name of a good mechanic, but there's no need to rush over to fix it.

Use technology to reduce in-person contact whenever possible. Use apps like Our Family Wizard or email for non-emergency communication to help prevent conflict and keep records if needed.

Focus on being a dependable parent. Show up when it's expected. Keep your promises. Make your support payments on time. Be consistent with rules and discipline. Your children need at least one parent they can fully trust.

LOVE AFTER DIVORCE: BUILDING RELATIONSHIPS THAT LAST

Mike thought he was ready to date again. Divorced for six months, he felt good about his custody arrangement and figured it was time to "get back out there." He downloaded three dating apps, went on twelve dates in two months, and found himself more confused and frustrated than when he started!

I kept thinking something was wrong with me, Mike told me during a coaching session. "These women seemed nice enough, but I had no idea what I was looking for. I was just dating to be dating, you know? It felt like I was trying to fill a hole instead of actually connecting with anyone."

Mike's experience is typical. Most divorced men approach dating the same way they handled everything else during their divorce - by reacting. They don't plan ahead. They jump back into dating because they're lonely, because their friends tell them to, or because they think they should, without taking the time to figure out who they are now and what they truly want.

The men who build strong, lasting relationships after divorce understand something crucial: dating after divorce isn't about finding someone to complete you or fix what's broken. It's about finding someone who enhances the life you've already rebuilt.

This fits perfectly in your stabilization phase. You're not rushing into dating as a way to escape loneliness or prove something to yourself or others. You're approaching it strategically, when you're ready, and as part of building your complete new life.

WHEN YOU'RE ACTUALLY READY TO DATE

Forget the timelines you read online. Forget your buddy telling you, "It's been long enough." And definitely forget what your ex is doing with her dating life. The only timeline that matters is yours, and readiness isn't about how much time has passed - it's about where you are, both emotionally and practically.

Being ready means you've done the tough work of understanding what went wrong in your marriage and what role you played. This doesn't mean berating yourself or accepting all the blame. It involves honestly examining your patterns, communication style, conflict management, and relationship skills.

Tom spent two years in therapy after his divorce, not because he was broken, but because he wanted to understand why he kept choosing women who weren't compatible with his long-term goals. "I realized I had a pattern of being attracted to women who needed fixing," he said. "I thought I was being helpful, but really I was avoiding dealing with my own stuff."

Ready means you can talk about your divorce without anger, bitterness, or the need to prove you were right. It means you can acknowledge both your mistakes and your ex's, doing so without needing to assign blame or play victim because you've moved from anger to acceptance, from reactive to strategic.

You Can Be Alone Without Being Lonely

I believe this is the most important point; the clearest sign you're ready to date is that you don't have to. You've built a life you genuinely enjoy. You have friends, interests, routines, and goals that bring you fulfillment. You're dating to share your life with someone, not because you need someone to give it meaning.

This doesn't mean you have to be perfectly content forever or that your life has to be perfect first. It means you've reached a point where another person would enhance your life rather than complete it. Carlos put it this way: "When I was ready to date again, I realized I didn't want just anyone - I wanted someone who would make my already good life even better. That's completely different from wanting someone to rescue me from loneliness."

Your Kids Are Stable

If you have children, their adjustment is a crucial factor in determining your readiness for dating. Kids need time to process the divorce and establish new routines. They need to feel secure in their relationship with you before you introduce the complexity of dating.

Most child psychologists recommend waiting at least six months to a year before introducing children to anyone you're dating, and much longer before serious relationships. Your children's emotional health takes precedence over your romantic life, period. However, these are not rules. Use common sense and your children's personality and maturity to determine what is best.

Red Flags: Learning From Your Past

The biggest advantage you have when dating after divorce is experience. You know pretty damn well what doesn't work! You've learned painful lessons about compatibility, communication, and conflict resolution. Use that knowledge wisely.

If you were married to someone who avoided conflict, pay attention to how potential partners handle disagreement. If your ex had addiction issues, notice how new people relate to alcohol, drugs, or other compulsive behaviors. If your marriage has suffered from financial irresponsibility, observe how people manage their money.

The goal isn't to find someone perfect - but you can certainly avoid repeating the same fundamental incompatibilities that destroyed your marriage.

Red Flags That Should End Things Immediately

Some behaviors should be automatic deal-breakers, regardless of how attracted you are or how much you want the relationship to work.

Anyone who pressures you to move faster than you're comfortable with - whether that's physical intimacy, meeting your children, or making commitments. Healthy people respect boundaries and timelines.

Anyone who speaks badly about all their exes or takes no responsibility for their past relationship failures - if everyone else was the problem, you'll be the next one.

Anyone who tries to isolate you from friends, family, or activities you enjoy - often an early sign of controlling behavior that will get worse over time.

Anyone with active addiction issues, untreated mental health problems, or ongoing legal/financial chaos - you're not a rehabilitation project, and you can't fix someone else's life.

Chemistry is essential, but compatibility determines whether relationships last — focus on finding someone whose values, life goals, communication style, and lifestyle actually match yours.

Ask yourself these questions about anyone you're considering seriously: Do we handle conflict in compatible ways? Do we have similar goals for the future? Do we share core values about money, family, and lifestyle? Do we bring out the best in each other, or create drama? Can we discuss difficult topics without it becoming a fight?

HOW TO DISCUSS YOUR DIVORCE

New partners will want to know about your divorce. That's understandable. How you handle these conversations reveals your emotional maturity and sets the tone for trust in the new relationship.

The Three-Stage Approach

Early Dating Stage: Keep it simple and factual. "I was married for X years, we have X children together, and we divorced in [year]. We maintain a business-like relationship focused on co-parenting."

Don't elaborate by going into detail they didn't ask for, assign blame, or get emotional. Save deeper conversations for when you know each other better.

Getting Serious Stage: Share more context about what you learned and how you've grown. "My marriage taught me a lot about what I need in a relationship and what I can do better as a partner. I learned that I need someone who communicates directly rather than avoiding conflict."

Focus on what you learned rather than what your ex did wrong. Show that you've done the work to understand your part and grow from it.

Committed Relationship Stage: Be honest about ongoing challenges and how you handle them. "co-parenting has its difficult moments, but we've established boundaries that work. My kids will always be a priority, and I've learned to balance that with building a healthy adult relationship."

Be clear about how your new relationship fits with your existing responsibilities and commitments.

Never badmouth your ex to new partners! It makes you look petty and suggests you'll do the same to them someday. Never share intimate details about your marriage or divorce proceedings. Never use your dating life to get back at your ex or make her jealous.

PROTECTING YOUR ASSETS AND INTERESTS

Dating after divorce requires financial and legal awareness that single men often don't consider.

Pre-Relationship Financial Boundaries

Keep your finances completely separate during the dating phase. Don't lend money, co-sign loans, or make major purchases together until you're married. Don't give anyone access to your accounts, credit cards, or financial information.

Be cautious about expensive dating! You don't need to spend a lot of money to have good dates, and anyone who expects expensive entertainment as a prerequisite for dating probably isn't compatible with your post-divorce financial priorities.

Protecting Your Divorce Settlement

Understand how remarriage could affect your divorce agreement. Some alimony arrangements terminate when you remarry. Some custody agreements include provisions related to new partners and children. Know what you agreed to and how new relationships might influence those agreements.

Prenuptial Considerations

If you're thinking about remarriage, a prenuptial agreement is usually a wise choice for divorced men. You've accumulated assets, set up child support obligations, and learned costly lessons about ending relationships that you probably don't want to repeat. A prenup isn't romantic, but neither is losing half your retirement savings for the second time. The right partner will understand that it's about protecting both of your interests.

BLENDED FAMILY DYNAMICS

If you're dating someone who also has children, you're looking at a blended family situation. This requires additional calculated decisions beyond just romantic compatibility.

The Brady Bunch Myth

Forget everything you think you know about blended families from TV. Real blended families are complex, require years to develop healthy dynamics, and succeed only when adults prioritize the children's adjustment over their own romantic timeline. Successful blended families happen slowly. Children need time to adjust to divorce before the variable of adding stepparents is introduced. They need to feel secure in their relationships with both biological parents before building relationships with stepparents.

When and How to Introduce Children

Wait until at least six months of serious dating have gone smoothly before any child introductions. When you do introduce them, start slow. A casual group activity, not a family dinner. Let relationships develop naturally, without forcing connection. Don't expect your children and your partner's children to become instant siblings! Don't expect your kids to love your new partner right away. Avoid taking sides when conflicts arise between your children and your partner.

Co-Parenting with Four Adults

When both partners have children from previous marriages, you're managing co-parenting relationships with four adults, plus however many children. This requires exceptional communication, boundary-setting, and patience.

Establish clear rules about discipline. Generally, biological parents handle discipline only for their own children, especially early in the relationship. Don't let your new partner discipline your children, and refrain from trying to discipline theirs.

Coordinate schedules carefully. Blended families often face multiple custody schedules, differing rules between households, and complex logistics. Use shared calendars and ensure clear communication to prevent conflicts.

SHIELD YOURSELF: THE DATING READINESS ASSESSMENT

But hold up, let's rewind here. Before you start dating seriously, honestly evaluate your readiness using these questions:

Can you describe what went wrong in your marriage without getting angry or defensive? Do you understand what patterns you want to change in future relationships?

Are you financially stable enough to date without it impacting your child support or your basic needs? Do you have a social life and interests that fulfill you outside of dating?

Have your children adjusted to the divorce and custody routine? Are you ready to maintain appropriate boundaries between your romantic life and your parenting responsibilities?

Can you manage rejection, disappointment, or relationship conflicts without losing your stability? Do you know what you want in a long-term partner, not just what you don't want?

Are you dating to improve an already good life, or to fix issues in your current life? Do you have realistic expectations about timelines for serious relationships and blended families?

If you can't answer yes to most of these questions, focus on building those foundations before jumping into dating. The right relationship will be worth waiting for.

BUILDING SYSTEMS FOR LONG-TERM SUCCESS

Smart men don't rely on motivation or willpower — they build systems that work regardless of how they feel on any given day.

During your stabilization phase, create systems that support your continued growth:

Create a morning routine that starts your day with purpose and energy. It doesn't have to be complicated — maybe it's just coffee, five minutes of planning your day, and checking in on your most important relationships.

Create a fitness routine you can stick to no matter what. This could be lifting weights twice a week, running every other day, or playing tennis on weekends. The main thing is being consistent, not perfect.

Create a financial system that automatically saves and invests your money. Set up automatic transfers for savings, automatic contributions to investments, and automatic bill payments. Make good financial decisions the easy choice by automating whenever possible.

Develop a personal growth system that ensures you're continuously improving. This might be reading one book per month, taking online courses, or working with a coach or therapist. Invest in becoming better, not just different.

SHIELD YOURSELF: THE QUARTERLY STABILIZATION CHECK

Every three months during your stabilization phase, honestly assess your progress in these key areas:

Physical Health: Am I stronger and healthier than I was three months ago? What specific improvements have I made to my fitness, sleep, or nutrition?

Financial Progress: Am I making measurable progress toward my financial goals? Is my emergency fund growing? Am I reducing debt or increasing income?

Career Development: Am I growing professionally, or just going through the motions? Have I learned new skills, built relationships, or taken on new challenges?

Relationships: Are my relationships with my children, friends, and family getting stronger? Am I building new connections and maintaining existing ones?

Co-parenting: Is my relationship with my ex-wife becoming more businesslike and less emotional? Are we working together better for the kids?

Personal Growth: Am I becoming a better version of myself, or just staying busy? What have I learned about myself in the past three months?

In any area where you're not making progress, identify one specific action you can take this week to move forward.

THE FOUNDATION FOR WHAT'S NEXT

You're not just surviving anymore. You're getting busy living, building the foundation for a life that won't just be different from your marriage — it will be better.

This stabilization phase can seem tedious, but it is crucial because it sets the stage for everything that comes next. Handle it well, and you'll have the solid ground necessary for real transformation. Rush through it or neglect it, and you'll struggle to build anything lasting.

Take your time with this phase. There's no deadline for when you have to start dating again or start making major life changes. Focus on becoming the kind of man who attracts the life he wants instead of chasing external changes before you're ready internally.

The goal isn't perfection — it's progress. Every system you create, every boundary you set, and every healthy choice you make is an investment in your future self. You're no longer just recovering from your divorce; you're preparing for everything that lies ahead.

ONE MOVE THAT MATTERS

This week, choose one area from this chapter and make one significant commitment to improve it over the next month.

If you choose fitness, sign up for a gym membership or martial arts classes and schedule your first three workouts.

If you pick finances, open a high-yield savings account and set up an automatic weekly transfer.

Relationships? Plan something special with your children or reach out to an old friend you've been meaning to reconnect with.

Career development? Dust off and update your LinkedIn profile, and message three professional contacts to set up coffee meetings.

Personal growth? Buy three books on a topic you're interested in learning about and schedule time to read them.

Dating? Well... complete an honest dating readiness assessment before proceeding. Write down what you learned from your marriage about compatibility, communication, and conflict resolution. Identify what you're looking for in a future partner, and what red flags you'll watch for. If you're not ready to date, that's completely fine! Instead, focus on one area that needs development - whether that's emotional processing, financial stability, or building your social life outside of dating. If you are ready to date, choose one specific step to take this week. This might include updating your online dating profile with recent photos, asking friends if they know anyone they'd recommend, or joining a social group where you can naturally meet compatible people.

Whatever you choose, make it specific and set a deadline. Stabilization isn't about dramatic overnight changes - it's about creating solid systems that support consistent, long-term growth.

Key Takeaways: The stabilization phase emphasizes building strong systems and foundations rather than making major changes. Focus on establishing consistent routines in fitness, finances, relationships, and personal growth. This structured approach to rebuilding creates a solid base necessary for long-term success and transformation. And remember, dating after divorce calls for strategic timing, clear boundaries, and realistic expectations. Concentrate on becoming the kind of man who attracts the right person to build a life with.

CHAPTER 17
THRIVING IN YOUR 2.0 LIFE

David stood at his son's high school graduation, proudly watching his kid accept an academic achievement award. As his ex-wife smiled and waved from across the auditorium, David felt something he hadn't experienced in years: complete peace. His business? Thriving. His health? The best it had been since his twenties. And his relationship with both his kids was stronger than it had ever been during his marriage.

> "You know what's crazy?" he told his friend later. "Five years ago, I thought my life was over. I was wrong. It was just beginning."

This is where everything comes together.

You've survived the crisis. You've stabilized the chaos. You've built and secured solid systems in every area of your life. Your kids are doing well. Your money situation is under control. Your career is surging forward. You've learned to be comfortable in your own skin again.

Now comes the exciting part - building a life that's not just better than your marriage, but better than anything you ever thought possible.

This is you, 2.0. You're not the same man who walked into that marriage all those years ago. You're not even the same man who walked out of it. You're the upgraded version — smarter, stronger, more purposeful, more authentic.

And honestly? You're just getting started.

MOVING FROM SURVIVOR TO CREATOR

Here's what separates the men who truly thrive from those who get by after divorce: their mindset.

The guys who merely survive keep asking, "How do I get back to where I was?"

Those who thrive ask, "What can I build now that I couldn't build before?"

That difference in thinking changes everything.

Sam figured this out after his divorce. He told me something that really stuck: "Getting divorced isn't a death sentence. My ex-wife and I decided to stop being married to each other. Now I'm happy, she's happy, my kids are happy. We're all happy." Notice what he didn't say? He didn't say, "I survived that damn divorce!" He said everyone's happier now. I'm a lawyer, not a therapist... but I am confident in saying that's not just surviving — that's strategic transformation.

When your kids see you building something better instead of mourning something broken, you teach them the most valuable lesson they'll ever learn: setbacks don't define you. How you respond to them does.

FINDING YOUR PURPOSE BEYOND YOURSELF

Tom's story illustrates what becomes possible when you discover genuine purpose after divorce. He was a successful business owner who lost everything in a bitter, drawn-out, bloody divorce battle. Instead of staying bitter, he spent three years rebuilding his life from scratch.

But Tom didn't stop at just getting back to where he was. He started mentoring other divorced fathers, sharing what he'd learned about rebuilding after loss. That mentoring evolved into speaking engagements, which in turn led to writing a book, ultimately opening doors he never expected.

"The divorce forced me to figure out who I really was and what I actually wanted," Tom explained. "I discovered I wanted to help other men avoid the mistakes I made. That purpose gave me energy I didn't have, even during my marriage."

Purpose isn't just about feeling good; it's about building something greater than yourself. When you center your life on helping others, everything else naturally falls into place.

CREATING WEALTH THAT LASTS

Your 2.0 life needs a financial foundation that can weather any storm. Seeing beyond that horizon means thinking beyond just replacing what you lost in the divorce. You want to build wealth that creates long-term options, freedom, and security.

Start by increasing your earning power. The skills that got you this far might not be enough for where you want to go. Consider additional training, certifications, or developing expertise in high-demand areas of your field.

Many divorced men discover entrepreneurial opportunities they never considered while married. Maybe it's consulting in your area of expertise, starting a side business, or investing in real estate. The key is cultivating multiple streams of income so you're not dependent on any single source.

Protect what you build by creating legal barriers around your assets. Work with both an attorney and a financial advisor to structure your wealth in a way that shields it from future risks. This isn't being paranoid - it's being smart.

Think about it this way: you've already been through one financial reset. Do you want to go through another one? Build systems that ensure your wealth grows consistently and stays protected.

BECOMING THE FATHER YOU WERE MEANT TO BE

It may not seem like it from media stereotypes, but one of the unexpected benefits of divorce is often becoming a better father. When you're not illustrating that it's acceptable to remain in an unhappy marriage, when you're showing your children what resilience looks like, and when you're demonstrating that life can be rebuilt from scratch - you become the father they need, not just the one they've got.

Create unique traditions with your kids. This could include Saturday morning hikes, teaching them to cook, working on projects together, or exploring new places. These memories will be cherished and might even be passed down to their children.

Be fully present when you're with them. No phones, no distractions, no thinking about work or your ex or anything else. Your time with them is precious - treat it that way.

Most importantly, let them see you grow. Don't hide your challenges from them completely but show them how you handle difficulties with grace and determination. They're learning how to be adults by watching you do it.

BUILDING RELATIONSHIPS THAT MATTER

Your 2.0 life needs relationships built on mutual respect and shared values, not just convenience or habit.

Start with friendships. Many divorced men quickly realize that their social life was entirely managed by their ex-wife. A cold, lonely realization and atrophied skillset? Yes. But also a blessing in disguise. Now, you get to choose friends based on who you actually want to spend time with, not on couple compatibility.

Look for men who share your interests and values. Join groups where you'll meet like-minded people - whether that's fitness classes, volunteer organizations, professional groups, or hobby clubs. The goal is to build real friendships that support who you're becoming.

If you're ready for a romantic relationship, approach it differently than you did before. You know more about yourself now. You know what you want and what you won't accept. Don't settle for someone who's just available - wait for someone who adds real, undeniable value to the life you've built.

Take your time with new relationships. You've put too much work into rebuilding your life to risk it on someone who isn't worth it. The right person will appreciate the strong foundation you've created and want to build something even better together.

MAINTAINING YOUR PHYSICAL AND MENTAL EDGE

Your 2.0 life requires 2.0 maintenance. The habits that got you healthy need to evolve right along with you.

Keep challenging your body as you age. Your fitness routine from your forties might not work in your fifties or sixties, but that doesn't mean you stop! It means you adapt. You could switch from heavy lifting to yoga, from running to swimming, from competitive sports to active hobbies. The key is staying physically capable and energetic.

Continue investing in your mental health as well. Therapy isn't a one-time fix — it's ongoing maintenance for your emotional well-being. Even when life is good, having someone to process challenges with keeps you sharp, self-aware, and protected from slipping back into old patterns.

Keep learning new things. Read books outside your comfort zone. Take courses in subjects that interest you. Travel to places that challenge your perspective. Your brain needs new experiences to stay flexible and creative.

DEVELOPING YOUR PROFESSIONAL LEGACY

Your career in your 2.0 life can be completely different from what came before. Many men use divorce as a catalyst to pursue work that actually fulfills them, rather than just paying the bills.

Perhaps you've always wanted to start your own business, but thought it was too risky while you're married. You may be now considering switching industries entirely. Perhaps you want to work less and enjoy life more or work more strategically to build substantial wealth.

The point is you get to choose. You're not locked into decisions you made twenty years ago that were based on someone else's priorities. You can build a career that aligns with the life you want, not just the one you were once confined to.

Consider how you want to be remembered professionally. What expertise do you want to develop? What problems do you want to solve? What impact do you want to have? Your professional legacy starts with the choices you make today.

CREATING SYSTEMS FOR CONTINUOUS GROWTH

Strategic men don't rely on motivation or willpower - they build systems that work regardless of how they feel on any given day.

Develop a personal development system that ensures continuous improvement. It could be reading one book per month, listening to educational podcasts during commutes, or attending industry conferences annually. The method matters less than the consistency with which you apply it.

Build a financial system that automatically grows your wealth. Automate it so wealth-building is the easy choice, not something you have to remember to do.

Develop a relationship system that maintains your important connections. Schedule regular check-ins with your children, plan quarterly activities with close friends, and set aside time for the relationships that matter most.

Design a health system that keeps you physically and mentally strong. Whether it's daily workouts, weekly meal prep, monthly health check-ups, or annual retreats - create routines that support your long-term well-being.

YOUR NEW RELATIONSHIP WITH YOUR EX

Here's something nobody talks about: your relationship with your ex-wife will likely improve dramatically once you build your 2.0 life! Not because she changes, but because you do.

When you're thriving instead of just surviving, you stop being triggered by her behavior. When you're happy in your own life, her opinions matter less. When you're financially stable, support payments don't sting as much. When you have purpose, her drama is like a fly buzzing around your kitchen, not a leaf blower in your bedroom.

To be clear, this isn't about impressing her or winning her back. It's about becoming so focused on your own growth that her presence in your life becomes purely practical - coordinating schedules. Nothing more.

The opposite of love isn't hate - it's healthy indifference. When you reach that point with your ex, you know you've truly moved on.

SHIELD YOURSELF: THE 2.0 LIFE ASSESSMENT

Conduct a strategic life assessment every six months. Be honest about your progress in these key areas:

Physical and Mental Health: Am I stronger, healthier, and more energetic than six months ago? What specific improvements have I made to my fitness, nutrition, sleep, or mental well-being?

Financial Growth: Is my net worth increasing? Am I building multiple income streams? Do I have adequate insurance and legal protections for my assets?

Career Development: Am I growing professionally, or just going through the motions? Have I developed new skills, built valuable relationships, or taken on meaningful challenges?

Relationships: Are my relationships with my children deepening? Do I have strong friendships that support who I'm becoming? If I'm dating, is it adding value to my life?

Purpose and Contribution: Do I have something that gets me excited about the future? Am I contributing to something bigger than myself? What legacy am I building?

Personal Growth: What have I learned about myself in the past six months? How have I challenged my thinking or stepped outside my comfort zone?

In any area where you're not progressing, identify one specific action you can take this week to get unstuck.

WHEN YOU KNOW YOU'VE MADE IT

You'll know you've successfully built your 2.0 life when certain things start happening naturally:

Your ex-wife's behavior doesn't trigger you anymore. Your children actively choose to spend extra time with you. People start asking you for advice about handling life challenges. You can't imagine going back to your old life, even if someone offered.

You wake up excited about your day more often than not. Money isn't a constant source of stress. You have friends who knew you before the divorce and friends who met you after. You're proud to introduce yourself as who you are now, not who you used to be.

Most importantly, you've stopped fantasizing about "getting back to normal" and started strategically thinking about "what's next?"

THE MESSAGE FOR YOUR FORMER SELF

If you could go back and talk to yourself at the beginning of this journey — sitting in that lawyer's office, feeling sweaty, scared, and confused… like your life was ending — what would you tell him?

This will be the hardest thing you've ever done, but also the most important. You'll discover strength you didn't know you had and build a life better than anything you believed was possible. Your kids will be okay—they'll be proud of who you become. The man you are now thinks this is the end, but you're actually just getting started.

YOUR LEGACY STARTS TODAY

Your 2.0 life isn't just about you. It's about the legacy you're creating with every choice you make, every habit you build, every relationship you nurture.

Your children are watching. They're learning what it means to be a man — not from your words, but from your actions. Show them that setbacks aren't permanent, that pain can turn into purpose, and that anyone can rebuild their life at any age, no matter the circumstances.

Your legacy isn't what you leave behind when you die - it's what you build every single day you're alive.

The man who entered his divorce and the man who valiantly emerged from it should be completely different people. Make sure that the difference represents the best version of who you were meant to become.

You've weathered the storm. You've stabilized in the calm. Now you get to build something magnificent.

Your 2.0 life is waiting. It's time to create it.

ONE MOVE THAT MATTERS

This week, identify one area of your 2.0 life that represents your next level of growth - advanced fitness goals, business opportunities, mentoring others, developing expertise, or creating something meaningful and lasting.

Make one specific commitment to advance in that area and set a clear deadline.

If you choose advanced fitness, sign up for a challenging event, such as a marathon or an obstacle race, and start training.

Business? Research one business idea and take the first concrete step toward realizing it.

Mentoring? Reach out to one man who could benefit from your experience and offer to help.

Expertise development? Commit to creating one piece of content — an article, video, or presentation — that shares your knowledge with others.

Legacy building? Start one project that will outlast you, whether that's teaching your skills to your children, volunteering for a cause you care about, or creating something valuable.

The best version of your life isn't built in earth-shattering, awe-inspiring, dramatic moments - it's small, consistent actions that compound over time.

Key Takeaways: Your 2.0 life isn't about recovery from divorce — it's about a renaissance. It's strategic growth. It's about approaching rebuilding with purpose rather than desperation, using crisis as a catalyst for improvement instead of an excuse for stagnation, and building systems that support ongoing development rather than just hoping things get better — you don't just survive divorce; you transform it into the foundation for the best years of your life. The goal isn't to return to who you were but to become who you were always meant to be.

CHAPTER 18
BUILDING LONG-TERM WEALTH AS A DIVORCED MAN

Two years after his divorce, Marcus was sitting in his financial advisor's office, reviewing his portfolio, when something hit him hard: for the first time in his adult life, he was building wealth for himself and his children, not just maintaining a lifestyle. His net worth had grown 40% since the divorce was finalized, his credit score was higher than it had ever been during his marriage, and he was on track to retire earlier than he'd ever thought possible!

"The weird thing is, I'm actually in better financial shape now than when I was married," Marcus told me. "When you're forced to be strategic about every dollar, you make smarter decisions. Plus, I'm not funding anyone else's spending habits."

Marcus found out what many divorced men realize: when they are strategic, single fathers can actually speed up wealth building instead of slowing it down after a divorce. You have full control over your financial choices, clear goals to aim for, and strong motivation in your children's future.

This chapter is about moving beyond financial recovery and into financial mastery. You've stabilized your situation, built your emergency fund, and established basic systems. Now it's time to build real wealth that gives you options and security you never had before. Note that I am not a financial expert, but having gone through a divorce, worked with hundreds of divorced men, and spoken with countless financial experts, there are common themes I have seen and heard over and over. You should always consult with financial experts to discuss your specific circumstances before engaging in any of the following ideas.

REBUILDING CREDIT TO UNLOCK OPPORTUNITIES

Your credit score is the foundation of wealth building. It determines the cost of major purchases like homes, cars, and business loans. Divorce often damages credit through joint accounts, temporary financial stress, and complex financial separations. But strategic credit rebuilding can happen faster than most men realize.

The 90-Day Credit Boost Strategy

It may feel like an embarrassing college student maneuver but start by becoming an authorized user on a family member's account with excellent credit and low utilization. This can boost your score 50–100 points within 60 days. You don't actually need access to the card — just the positive payment history showing on your report.

Pay down existing credit cards strategically, focusing on utilization ratios rather than just total debt. Getting a card from 80% utilization to 30% helps your score more than paying off a smaller balance elsewhere. If you have a $5,000 limit, keep the balance below $500 for optimal scoring.

Set up automatic payments for everything — not just the minimum, but the full balances on all credit cards — and ensure on-time payments for all bills. Payment history is 35% of your score, and even one late payment can drop you 60–100 points overnight.

The Strategic Rebuild Timeline

Jason rebuilt his credit from 580 to 740 in 18 months after his divorce. "I treated credit repair like a part-time job," he said. "I disputed every error, paid down cards strategically, and opened new accounts slowly. The improvement was dramatic once I understood how scoring actually works."

Most divorced men can significantly improve their credit score within a year with consistent effort. This improvement unlocks better mortgage rates, business loans, and investment opportunities that can save or earn you tens of thousands over time.

INVESTMENT STRATEGIES FOR SINGLE-INCOME HOUSEHOLDS

Traditional investment advice assumes dual incomes and shared financial goals. As a single father, you therefore need a different playbook that accounts for your unique situation and responsibilities.

The Single Father's Investment Hierarchy

Before investing beyond retirement accounts, ensure adequate insurance protection. Your children depend on your income alone, making disability and life insurance even more critical than for married men. Term life insurance should cover 10-12 times your annual income, rather than the typical 6–8 times recommended for dual-income households.

Maximize tax-advantaged accounts first, but with a twist. Single fathers often benefit more from Roth 401(k) and Roth IRA contributions because their current tax rate might be higher than their retirement rate, especially if they're in a high-earning phase now.

Consider 529 college savings plans for each child, but don't prioritize these over retirement savings. Fund your retirement first, then help with college. Your children can borrow for education, but you can't borrow for retirement.

Asset Allocation for Single Fathers

Single-income households need more conservative portfolios than dual-income families. A major market downturn right before college expenses or right before retirement is made all the more devastating when you can't rely on a spouse's income to smooth things over.

Consider keeping 25–30% of your portfolio in bonds or conservative investments, even though this is higher than typical age-based recommendations. Use target-date funds if you're not comfortable with active allocation but choose a target date 5–10 years after your planned retirement to ensure slightly more conservative positioning.

Dollar-cost averaging works very well for single fathers because it helps smooth out market fluctuations and aligns with consistent monthly investing from your single paycheck. Set up automatic investments to remove emotion from the process.

Tax-Efficient Investing

Single fathers often face higher tax rates than married couples, making tax efficiency crucial. Keep tax-inefficient investments, such as REITs and bonds, in tax-advantaged accounts. Hold index funds and individual stocks in taxable accounts where they receive favorable tax treatment.

Consider tax-loss harvesting in taxable accounts to offset gains. Many brokerages offer automatic tax-loss harvesting that can save hundreds or thousands annually, all without any effort on your part.

TAX STRATEGY CHANGES THAT BUILD WEALTH

Divorce fundamentally changes your tax situation, creating opportunities and challenges that can significantly impact wealth building.

Filing Status Optimization

Your filing status changes from married filing jointly to single or head of household. While being the head of household provides better tax rates and higher standard deductions, it also requires paying more than half the costs of maintaining a home where a qualifying child lives for more than half the year.

Child tax credits and dependent exemptions typically go to the custodial parent, but this can be negotiated. The custodial parent can release exemptions to the non-custodial parent using IRS Form 8332, often in exchange for the non-custodial parent paying specific expenses or higher support.

Alimony Tax Implications

For divorces finalized after December 31, 2018, alimony payments are no longer tax-deductible for the payer or taxable for the recipient. This means you're paying alimony with after-tax dollars, therefore making it effectively more expensive than under the old rules.

If you're receiving alimony under the new rules, this non-taxable income doesn't count toward IRA contribution limits either, potentially reducing your ability to save for retirement. Plan accordingly by maximizing employer retirement plan contributions.

Strategic Tax Planning Moves

Consider Roth conversions during years when your income is lower due to temporary financial changes resulting from divorce. Converting traditional IRA funds to Roth accounts during lower-income years can result in significant tax savings over the long term.

Maximize business deductions if you're self-employed or have side income. And don't forget about home office deductions, business equipment, and professional development expenses, as they can all significantly reduce taxable income.

BUILDING WEALTH DESPITE CHILD SUPPORT OBLIGATIONS

Child support obligations don't have to prevent wealth building - they just require different strategies that work within your modified cash flow.

The Net Worth Focus Approach

Instead of focusing only on income, concentrate on net worth growth. Many divorced men increase their net worth faster than married men because they make more strategic financial decisions and retain complete control over spending.

Track your net worth monthly using apps like Personal Capital or Mint. Seeing your wealth grow despite support obligations provides motivation and helps you make more informed decisions based on long-term impact rather than short-term cash flow.

Automated Wealth Building

Set up automatic transfers immediately after payday, before you can spend the money on discretionary items. Even $200–300 per month invested consistently builds substantial wealth over time, through compound growth.

Create separate savings goals for different purposes: emergency fund, children's activities, vacation fund, and investment account. This prevents you from raiding long-term savings for short-term expenses.

HIGH-IMPACT MOVES

Refinance your mortgage if rates have dropped since your divorce. The payment reduction can free up hundreds per month for investing. Similarly, refinance or pay off high-interest debt to redirect those payments toward wealth building.

Consider house hacking - renting out a room or basement to generate additional income. This extra income can accelerate debt payoff or investment contributions significantly.

Look for ways to increase income through side businesses, consulting, or career advancement. Even an extra $500 monthly can add $100,000+ to your net worth over 10–15 years when invested diligently.

CAREER PIVOTS THAT ACCELERATE WEALTH

Divorce often provides the freedom to make career changes that were impossible during marriage and which can dramatically accelerate wealth building.

The Strategic Career Assessment

Evaluate the wealth-building potential of your current career path. Are you in a field with strong income growth prospects? Do you have opportunities for advancement, business ownership, or establishing additional income streams? Consider careers or side businesses that scale with your existing skills. A marketing professional might start a consulting practice, a teacher might develop online courses, or a tradesman might start a contracting business.

Skills That Pay Premium Wages

Technology skills consistently command premium wages and often allow remote work, giving you more time with your children. Consider acquiring high-value skills such as data analysis, digital marketing, or software development through online courses. Sales skills are transferable across industries and often offer unlimited income potential through commissions. Many divorced men find success in real estate, insurance, or business-to-business (B2B) sales, where the relationship skills and life experience gained during the divorce process provide an advantage.

Business Ownership Considerations

Starting a business after divorce can accelerate wealth building, but requires careful planning around child support obligations and custody schedules. Many courts look at business income differently from W-2 income in their support calculations. Consider businesses that can accommodate your custody schedule, or those that involve your children when appropriate. Many successful divorced fathers start businesses in areas such as coaching, consulting, or service-based companies that offer flexible scheduling options.

SHIELD YOURSELF: WEALTH BUILDING ASSESSMENT

Use this assessment to evaluate your wealth-building progress and identify areas for improvement:

Do you have a clear picture of your net worth? Do you track it regularly? Are you maximizing all available tax-advantaged investment accounts before investing in taxable accounts?

Is your credit score above 740, enabling you to get the best rates on mortgages and business loans? Do you have adequate insurance protection relative to your single-income household status?

Are you building wealth despite support obligations, or just maintaining your current financial position? Do you have a clear 5–10 year financial plan that accounts for children's expenses and your retirement goals?

Are you considering career moves or additional income streams that could accelerate wealth building? Do you understand the tax implications of your divorce and are you optimizing accordingly?

If you answered no to several questions, focus on those areas first. Effective wealth building requires systematic progress across multiple areas, not perfection in just one.

ONE MOVE THAT MATTERS

This week, choose one high-impact wealth-building action and commit to completing it within 30 days.

If your credit needs improvement, consider signing up for Credit Karma or a similar monitoring service, reviewing your reports, disputing any errors, and setting up automatic payments for all bills. If you're not maximizing retirement accounts, calculate how much you can contribute and set up automatic increases to do so.

If you need a better investment allocation, schedule a consultation with a fee-only financial advisor who understands the complexities of divorce situations. If your career needs evaluation, research salary data for your field and identify three specific skills or certifications to bolster your earning potential.

If you're not tracking net worth, set up accounts with Personal Capital or Mint and input all your assets and debts to establish a baseline. If you need additional income streams, research three potential side businesses or consulting opportunities that match your skills and schedule.

The key is taking action this week, not just planning to take action someday. Wealth building accelerates through consistent action, not perfect planning.

Key Takeaways: Building long-term wealth as a single father requires different strategies than those typically recommended for married couples. Focus on credit optimization, tax-efficient investing, strategic career moves, and systematic wealth building compatible with your support obligations. Single fathers who approach wealth building strategically often build their net worth faster than their married counterparts because they make more intentional financial decisions and have complete control over their financial future. The goal isn't just financial recovery - it's financial independence, which provides you and your children with security and greater life options.

Note: Consult a financial expert before implementing any new financial plan.

CHAPTER 19
CONCLUSION

You made it.

Not just through this book, but on the other side of one of life's most challenging experiences. You've learned that divorce doesn't have to destroy you, and that it can actually be the catalyst for becoming the man you were always meant to be.

WHAT YOU'VE ACCOMPLISHED

Look at how far you've come since the beginning of this book! Perhaps you were still reeling when you picked this up, blindsided by divorce, unprepared for what was coming, possibly feeling like a victim of circumstances beyond your control.

Now you understand how to recognize warning signs before they become disasters. You know how to build a professional team that works in your interests. You've learned to protect your money, your children, your freedom, and your sanity through strategic planning rather than knee-jerk, regrettable — and EXPENSIVE — emotional reactions.

You've come to understand the difference between fighting smart and fighting hard. You know how to negotiate from a place of quiet strength rather than bitter desperation. You can create agreements that actually work in real life, not just on paper.

Most importantly, you've discovered that your post-divorce life can be even brighter than anything you had before—if you approach it diligently, with the right strategy.

THE SKILLS YOU'VE DEVELOPED

The strategies and mindset shift you've learned aren't just for surviving divorce. They're core life skills that will serve you for decades to come.

You've learned to document systematically rather than rely on memory when it matters. You know how to think systematically about long-term consequences rather than making impulsive decisions based on short-term emotions. You understand and value investing in professional guidance instead of trying to figure everything out on your own.

You've developed the ability to separate what you can control from what you can't, focus your energy on what actually makes a difference, and let the rest fall away. You know how to build systems that support your success, rather than hoping things will work out.

These skills apply to every aspect of your life, including your career, relationships, health, and financial future. You've become a more strategic man, and the benefits of that transformation will grow over the years and generations to come.

YOUR UNEXPECTED STRENGTHS

Many men discover strengths they didn't know they had during this process. You might have found that you're more resilient than you thought. You may have learned that you can handle difficult conversations, make tough decisions, and stand up for your interests even when it's uncomfortable.

You've probably become a better father than you were as a married man. When you're more present, more intentional, more aware of time's value, your children benefit. They see you handling adversity with dignity, purpose, and serenity - from that, they learn that setbacks aren't permanent and that people can rebuild their lives at any age.

You've likely developed better friendships because you're more authentic now. You're more willing to be vulnerable, ask for help, and be more gracious and grateful when receiving that genuine support. The relationships you build from this point on will be based on who you really are, not who you thought you should be.

You may go on to become one of the many men who also find renewed career success they never imagined because they're no longer playing it safe. You're not accepting "good enough" anymore. You're not afraid to take calculated risks or make necessary changes. Crisis has a way of clarifying priorities and accelerating growth when you approach it strategically.

A PERSONAL MESSAGE

I want you to know something important: **I'm proud of you.**

I'm proud that you chose to educate yourself rather than stumble through blindly. I'm proud that you invested in strategy rather than crossing your fingers and hoping for luck. I'm proud that you protected your children's interests, even when it was difficult. I'm proud that you maintained your integrity while securing your future.

Most men don't make such wise choices. Most men tend to react emotionally, avoid making difficult decisions, and hope someone else will swoop in and solve their problems. But you did the work. You made the hard choices. You invested in becoming the man your situation required.

The result: You didn't just avoid getting screwed by divorce - you excelled and did it strategically.

YOUR LEGACY STARTS NOW

Your children are watching and learning, seeing what it means to handle life's biggest challenges with your head held high. They're learning that failure isn't final, that people can rebuild, that calculated decisions wins over reflexive reactions.

The example you're setting will influence them for the rest of their lives. When they face their own difficult situations — and they will — they'll remember watching their father navigate divorce with purpose and dignity. They'll have a model for handling adversity that serves them well.

You'll also get the chance to support other men facing challenges similar to those you've overcome. Your experience can help others avoid making costly mistakes. When you share what you've learned, you'll amplify the impact of your own difficult journey.

YOUR NEXT CHAPTER

This book is coming to a close, but your strategic life is only just beginning. Here's what comes next:

Keep growing. Keep learning. Never stop improving and building. The moment you think you've "arrived" is when you start sliding backward. Stay curious about new opportunities and challenges.

Build something extraordinary with your freedom, wisdom, and resources. Something meaningful that will outlast you. Whether it's in your career, relationships, community involvement, or personal projects, let this experience serve as the cornerstone for something significant.

Stay connected with the professionals who helped you succeed. They understand your journey and can guide you through future challenges. Maintain those relationships, even when you don't think you need them.

Document your success and transformation. When tough days arrive — and they will — you'll need reminders of how far you've come and everything you've overcome. Keep track of your growth and achievements.

FINAL PROMISES

To Yourself: Promise never again to accept less than you deserve. You've learned your worth the hard way, built it even higher than ever, and developed the skills to protect it. Don't settle for mediocrity in any area of your life.

To Your Children: Promise to continue modeling resilience, calculated decisions, and integrity. They're establishing their own life patterns based on the example you set. Show them what's possible when someone approaches challenges with intelligence and determination.

To Other Men: Promise to share what you've learned when appropriate opportunities arise. Your story can inspire others to choose strategy over surrender. You don't have to become a counselor, but you can be the friend who offers honest, rock-solid guidance rather than just hollow sympathy.

To Your Future: Promise to have this experience serve as the root of something extraordinary you'll grow, rather than just putting it behind you. This isn't something that happened to you — it's something you strategically conquered.

THE ULTIMATE TRUTH

Here's what I know after guiding hundreds of men through this process:

Divorce is crushingly heavy. It causes facades to crack, can turn who you thought you were to dust, and reveals who you really are under pressure. Some men crumble beneath its weight. Others emerge stronger than they ever imagined possible.

You chose to emerge stronger.

You got divorced without getting screwed. Not through luck, manipulation, or someone else's generosity, but through careful planning and consistent execution. You approached one of life's most difficult transitions like the intelligent, capable man you are.

The strategies, tools, and mindset you've developed here will benefit you for many years. You've learned to think long-term, seek professional guidance, document systematically, and base decisions on logic rather than emotion. These are the qualities of successful people in any field.

A FINAL CHALLENGE

Share this book with someone who needs these strategies. Don't just recommend it — actually give him your copy or buy him one. Be the friend who rolls up his sleeves, gets involved, and offers real help instead of just sympathy.

Together, we can change the narrative about men and divorce — one strategic success at a time.

Years from now, when you're thriving in ways you can't imagine today, remember this moment. Remember that you chose strategy over emotion. Remember how you invested in growth rather than accepting victimhood. Remember that you protected what mattered most while building something far better.

Your children will remember, too. They'll remember watching their father unwaveringly face one of life's toughest challenges with dignity and discipline, emerging stronger. They'll carry those lessons throughout their lives, passing your upstanding, strategic mindset to the next generation.

That's your real legacy: not just surviving divorce but demonstrating how to handle adversity strategically.

Stay strong. Stay strategic. Stay unstoppable.

The best is yet to come,

— *John Nachlinger*

APPENDICES

APPENDIX A: DIVORCE DOCUMENT CHECKLIST

When divorce begins, the man with organized documents has an immediate strategic advantage. Courts and attorneys operate on paperwork — the more you can provide quickly, the faster and cheaper your case can proceed.

Use this comprehensive checklist to gather and organize your records. Create digital folders with subfolders by category for easy access.

FINANCIAL DOCUMENTS (PAST 5-7 YEARS)

Income Records:

- Tax returns (federal and state)
- W-2 forms and 1099s
- Pay stubs (most recent 6 months minimum)
- Business financial statements (if self-employed)
- Partnership/corporate tax returns
- Investment income statements
- Social Security benefits statements
- Disability or unemployment benefits documentation
- Pension or retirement income records

Bank and Investment Accounts:

- Checking account statements (all accounts, 12+ months)
- Savings account statements (all accounts, 12+ months)
- Investment account statements (stocks, bonds, mutual funds)
- Retirement account statements (401(k), IRA, pension)
- Business account statements (if applicable)
- Certificates of deposit
- Money market accounts
- Safe deposit box inventories

Debt and Liability Records:

- Mortgage statements and documents
- Home equity loan documents
- Credit card statements (all cards, 12+ months)
- Auto loan documents
- Student loan statements
- Personal loan agreements
- Business debt documentation
- Medical debt records
- Tax liens or judgments

Real Estate Documentation:

- Property deeds
- Mortgage documents and payment history
- Property tax assessments and payments
- Home insurance policies
- Rental property income/expense records
- Real estate purchase/sale agreements
- Home improvement receipts (major projects)

CHILD-RELATED DOCUMENTATION

Custody and Care Records:

- Children's birth certificates

- Adoption papers (if applicable)
- School enrollment and attendance records
- Medical records and insurance information
- Child care expenses and provider information
- Extracurricular activity costs and schedules
- Tutoring or special education expenses

Parenting Evidence:

- Photos of time spent with children
- School event attendance records
- Medical appointment participation
- Activity coaching or volunteer records
- Travel documentation with children
- Communication records about children's needs

PERSONAL AND LEGAL DOCUMENTS

Identification and Legal Papers:

- Birth certificates (yours and children's)
- Social Security cards
- Passports
- Driver's licenses
- Marriage certificate
- Prenuptial or postnuptial agreements
- Existing court orders (custody, support, restraining orders)
- Immigration documents (if applicable)

Insurance Documentation:

- Life insurance policies (cash value statements)
- Health insurance policies and coverage details
- Disability insurance policies
- Auto insurance policies
- Homeowner's or renter's insurance
- Umbrella or excess liability policies

BUSINESS DOCUMENTATION (IF APPLICABLE)

Business Financial Records:

- Articles of incorporation or partnership agreements
- Business tax returns (5–7 years)
- Profit and loss statements
- Balance sheets
- Business bank account statements
- Business loan documents
- Professional licenses
- Business valuations (if available)

STRATEGIC ORGANIZATION TIPS

Digital Organization: Scan physical documents and organize them into folders labeled by category and date. Use cloud storage for backup so you can access files from anywhere.

Physical Backup: Keep organized physical copies in a secure location away from home (e.g., a safety deposit box or a trusted family member's home).

Regular Updates: Update financial documents monthly during divorce proceedings. Courts often require current information.

Professional Copies: Make multiple copies of everything. Your attorney, mediator, and financial experts will need their own sets.

APPENDIX B: STATE-SPECIFIC DIVORCE RESOURCES

Important Disclaimer: Divorce laws differ greatly by state and frequently change. This appendix offers general guidance only. Always consult with a qualified family law attorney in your specific jurisdiction for up-to-date legal requirements and tailored strategic advice.

GENERAL STATE LAW VARIATIONS

Community Property vs. Equitable Distribution:

Community Property States: Arizona, California, Idaho, Louisiana, Nevada, New Mexico, Texas, Washington, Wisconsin. In these states, most assets acquired during marriage are considered equally owned by both spouses.

Equitable Distribution States: All other states divide marital property based on "fairness" rather than equal splits, considering factors like income, contributions, and future needs.

Residency Requirements: Most states require 3–12 months of residency before filing for divorce. Some require residency in specific counties as well.

Waiting Periods: Many states impose waiting periods between filing and finalization, ranging from 30 days to 6 months.

KEY RESOURCES BY REGION

Northeast Region:

- Court websites typically provide forms, filing requirements, and local rules
- Many states offer self-help centers with basic guidance
- Legal aid organizations assist low-income individuals

Southeast Region:

- Most states have mandatory mediation for cases involving children
- Parenting classes often required before custody orders
- Some states have simplified procedures for uncontested divorces

Midwest Region:

- Generally conservative approach to custody and support
- Strong emphasis on maintaining child relationships with both parents
- Many states offer collaborative divorce options

Western Region:

- Often more progressive in custody arrangements
- Many states recognize domestic partnerships
- Generally favorable to prenuptial agreements

FINDING CURRENT INFORMATION

Official Court Websites: Search "[Your State] family court" for official forms, procedures, and local rules.

State Bar Associations: Most offer attorney referral services and consumer legal information.

Legal Aid Organizations: Provide assistance for qualified low-income individuals.

Self-Help Centers: Many court systems offer basic legal guidance and form preparation assistance.

PROFESSIONAL LICENSING VERIFICATION

Always verify attorney licensing through your state bar association website. Look for:

- Current active license status
- Disciplinary history
- Areas of specialization
- Continuing education compliance

APPENDIX C: SAMPLE PARENTING PLANS THAT WORK

Legal Disclaimer: These are only sample frameworks, not legal templates. Since every family situation is different, always consult qualified family law professionals to develop plans suited to your specific circumstances and state laws.

50/50 PARENTING TIME ARRANGEMENTS

Week-on/Week-off Schedule:

- Child lives with each parent for seven consecutive days
- Exchange typically every Sunday evening or Monday morning
- Works best for school-aged children with cooperative parents
- Provides extended time for bonding and consistency

2–2-3 Rotation Schedule:

- Parent A: Monday-Tuesday
- Parent B: Wednesday-Thursday

- Alternating parent: Friday-Sunday
- Rotates weekly so neither parent always has weekends
- Better for younger children who need more frequent contact

Extended Summer Arrangements:

- Each parent gets 2–4 consecutive weeks in summer
- 60 days advance notice typically required
- Must consider camp schedules and family vacations
- Often includes makeup time during school year

PRIMARY CUSTODY WITH PARENTING TIME

Every Other Weekend Schedule:

- Non-primary parent: Friday 6:00 PM through Sunday 6:00 PM
- Alternating weekends provide regular contact
- Often includes one midweek dinner or overnight
- Standard arrangement in many jurisdictions

Midweek Contact:

- Tuesday or Wednesday evening dinner (3–4 hours)
- Or overnight midweek visit with return to school
- Maintains parent-child connection between weekends
- Requires proximity for school logistics

HOLIDAY AND VACATION PROVISIONS

Major Holiday Rotation:

- Christmas/Winter Break: Alternating years, often split
- Thanksgiving: Alternating years
- Spring Break: Alternating years or shared
- Memorial Day/Labor Day: Often linked to regular schedule

Birthday Celebrations:

- Child's birthday: 2–4 hours with non-custodial parent
- Mother's Day/Father's Day: With respective parent
- Parent birthdays: Often 2–4 hours, if desired

Summer Vacation Time:

- Each parent typically gets 1–4 weeks
- Must provide advance notice (30–90 days)
- Cannot interfere with other parent's vacation time
- Travel restrictions may apply (state/country limitations)

ESSENTIAL PLAN COMPONENTS

Pickup and Drop-off Procedures:

- Specific times and locations
- Who provides transportation
- What to do if running late
- Neutral location options for high-conflict cases

Communication Protocols:

- Phone/video call schedules with children
- How parents communicate about children
- Emergency contact procedures
- School communication responsibilities

Decision-Making Authority:

- Educational decisions (school choice, tutoring, special education)
- Medical decisions (routine vs. emergency care)
- Religious upbringing
- Extracurricular activities and associated costs

Expense Responsibilities:

- Child support amount and payment method
- Healthcare costs and insurance responsibility
- Activity fees and equipment costs
- College expense provisions (if desired)

SPECIAL CIRCUMSTANCES PROVISIONS

Relocation Procedures:

- Notice requirements for moves (typically 60–90 days)
- Distance limitations requiring court approval
- Modification procedures for custody/visitation
- Transportation responsibility changes

High-Conflict Safeguards:

- All communication through written methods (email/app)
- No direct contact between parents
- Neutral pickup/drop-off locations
- Specific behavior guidelines

Modification Procedures:

- Circumstances requiring court approval
- Mediation requirements before court action
- Notice procedures for requesting changes
- Annual review options

APPENDIX D: FINANCIAL RECOVERY ROADMAP

Divorce often disrupts finances, at least temporarily, but the right strategic rebuilding approach can lead to better financial health than you had during marriage. This roadmap offers a systematic way to recover financially and build wealth.

PHASE 1: STABILIZATION (FIRST 90 DAYS)

Immediate Financial Setup:

- Open individual checking and savings accounts in your name only
- Redirect payroll deposits to new accounts
- Apply for credit cards in your name only (maintain good credit)
- Obtain copies of all credit reports (Equifax, Experian, TransUnion)

Essential Budget Creation:

- Housing: Maximum 28–30% of gross income
- Transportation: Maximum 15–20% of gross income
- Food: Maximum 10–15% of gross income
- Insurance: Health, auto, renters/homeowner's
- Support obligations: As legally required

- Emergency fund building: Build what you can, even $25–50 per month is a good start

Debt Management:

- List all debts with balances, minimum payments, interest rates
- Prioritize high-interest debt elimination
- Negotiate payment plans if necessary
- Avoid taking on new debt except for housing/transportation

Legal Financial Protections:

- Close joint credit accounts if possible
- Remove spouse from authorized user status on your accounts
- Change beneficiaries on all accounts and insurance policies
- Update will and estate planning documents

PHASE 2: FOUNDATION BUILDING (3-12 MONTHS)

Emergency Fund Development:

- Target: 1–3 months of living expenses initially
- Use automatic transfers to build consistency
- Keep in high-yield savings account for accessibility
- Separate from other savings goals

Credit Rebuilding:

- Pay all bills on time (payment history = 35% of credit score)
- Keep credit utilization - below 30%, ideally below 10%
- Don't close old accounts (length of credit history matters)
- Consider secured credit cards if credit is damaged

Retirement Restart:

- Resume 401(k) contributions at least to employer match
- Open IRA if not already available
- Catch-up contributions if over 50
- Target 10–15% of income eventually

Insurance Evaluation:

- Health insurance through employer or marketplace
- Adequate life insurance for children's protection
- Disability insurance (often overlooked, but critical)
- Umbrella policy if you have significant assets

PHASE 3: GROWTH PHASE (1-3 YEARS)

Advanced Emergency Fund:

- Build to 6 months of living expenses
- Consider money market accounts for better returns
- Keep accessible but separate from investment accounts

Investment Diversification:

- Low-cost index fund portfolios
- Target-date funds for simplicity
- Dollar-cost averaging for consistency
- Avoid individual stock picking and speculation

Housing Decisions:

- Rent vs. buy analysis based on your situation
- Consider maintenance, taxes, and transaction costs
- Don't rush into homeownership for emotional reasons
- Ensure housing payment stays within budget guidelines

Income Optimization:

- Negotiate salary increases annually
- Develop additional income streams (consulting, side business)
- Invest in education/training for career advancement
- Network actively for opportunity development

PHASE 4: WEALTH BUILDING (3+ YEARS)

Advanced Investment Strategies:

- Maximize retirement account contributions
- Taxable investment accounts for additional growth
- Real estate investment consideration (if appropriate)
- Business ownership or partnership opportunities

Estate Planning Updates:

- Comprehensive will reflecting current wishes
- Appropriate trust structures for asset protection
- Power of attorney and healthcare directives
- Regular beneficiary updates on all accounts

Children's Financial Future:

- 529 college savings plans
- Teaching financial literacy to children
- Considering children in investment and insurance decisions
- Balancing current needs with future educational costs

Financial Independence Planning:

- Calculate retirement needs based on desired lifestyle
- Develop multiple income streams for security
- Consider early retirement strategies if desired
- Plan for potential healthcare costs in retirement

KEY FINANCIAL RATIOS TO TRACK

Debt-to-Income Ratio: Keep total debt payments below 36% of gross income

Savings Rate: Target 10–20% of income for long-term goals

Net Worth Growth: Track quarterly; should increase consistently over time

Emergency Fund Coverage: Maintain 3–6 months of expenses in accessible accounts

PROFESSIONAL FINANCIAL TEAM

Fee-Only Financial Planner: Comprehensive planning without product sales conflict of interest

CPA or Tax Professional: Optimize tax strategies and ensure compliance

Estate Planning Attorney: Protect assets and ensure proper wealth transfer

Insurance Agent: Adequate coverage without over-insuring

STRATEGIC FINANCIAL MINDSET

Long-Term Perspective: Wealth building is a marathon, not a sprint

Consistency Over Perfection: Regular contributions matter more than perfect timing

Education Investment: Financial literacy pays dividends for life

Professional Guidance: Strategic advice prevents expensive mistakes

APPENDIX E: THE DIVORCE SHIELD METHOD QUICK REFERENCE

This quick reference guide summarizes the core strategies from each phase of the divorce process for easy implementation and review.

PHASE 1: RECOGNITION AND PREPARATION

Warning Signs Checklist:

- Emotional distance or indifference from spouse
- Secretive behavior with phone/computer/mail
- New, unexplained expenses or financial activity
- Changes in work schedule or social patterns
- Conversations about "what if" scenarios
- Consulting with friends who've divorced
- Legal consultation without your knowledge

Immediate Protection Actions:

1. Begin discreet documentation of concerning behaviors
2. Gather and secure copies of all financial documents
3. Photograph valuable personal property
4. Establish individual email account for sensitive communications
5. Research family law attorneys in your area
6. Begin building emergency cash reserves

PHASE 2: FOUR PILLARS IMPLEMENTATION

Pillar 1 - Protecting Your Money:

- Document all income sources and variations
- Inventory all assets and debts completely
- Establish individual banking relationships
- Create post-divorce budget projections
- Protect business interests, if applicable
- Plan for support obligation scenarios

Pillar 2 - Protecting Your Children:

- Document all parenting activities daily
- Build relationships with schools and activity leaders
- Maintain consistent involvement in children's lives
- Photograph time spent with children
- Keep records of support provided
- Adjust work schedule to maximize availability

Pillar 3 - Protecting Your Freedom:

- Learn recording laws in your state
- Document any concerning behaviors from spouse
- Avoid situations that could be misinterpreted
- Maintain professional demeanor in all interactions
- Create emergency safety plans, if needed
- Build witness support for your character

Pillar 4 - Protecting Your Sanity:

- Establish regular exercise routine
- Build support network of friends/family
- Consider individual therapy for strategic guidance
- Maintain healthy eating and sleep habits
- Limit alcohol consumption during proceedings
- Practice stress management techniques

PHASE 3: TEAM BUILDING AND STRATEGY

Attorney Selection Criteria:

- Family law specialization (not general practice)
- Local court experience and relationships
- Communication style that matches your needs
- Fee structure you can afford long-term
- Track record with cases similar to yours
- Availability for strategy discussions

Additional Team Members:

- Therapist for emotional processing and strategy
- Financial advisor for asset protection planning
- CPA for tax implications of settlement options
- Business valuator if business interests involved
- Parenting coordinator for high-conflict cases

PHASE 4: NEGOTIATION AND RESOLUTION

Pre-Negotiation Strategy:

- Define your actual needs vs. wants clearly
- Research realistic settlement ranges for your situation
- Prepare supporting documentation for all positions
- Consider long-term consequences of each decision
- Identify areas where compromise serves your interests
- Plan responses to likely counteroffers

Negotiation Best Practices:

- Focus on interests rather than positions
- Maintain professional demeanor, regardless of provocation
- Document all agreements immediately in writing
- Avoid negotiating when emotionally triggered
- Consider mediation before litigation, when possible
- Keep children's interests paramount in all decisions

Settlement Evaluation Criteria:

- Financial impact over 5–10 years, not just immediate costs
- Effect on relationship with children long-term
- Enforceability of proposed terms
- Tax implications of asset divisions
- Ability to comply with ongoing obligations
- Comparison to likely court-ordered outcomes

PHASE 5: AGREEMENT FINALIZATION

Critical Agreement Elements:

- Specific rather than vague language throughout
- Clear enforcement mechanisms for violations
- Modification procedures for changed circumstances
- Detailed parenting time schedules and procedures
- Precise financial obligations and payment methods
- Built-in consequences that don't require court action

Final Review Process:

- Read entire agreement aloud to test comprehension
- Have attorney explain any unclear provisions
- Verify all financial calculations independently
- Ensure all verbal agreements are included in writing
- Confirm compliance deadlines and procedures
- Schedule follow-up review after implementation

PHASE 6: POST-DIVORCE RECOVERY AND BUILDING

First Year Priorities:

- Establish new routines for children and yourself
- Focus on co-parenting communication improvement
- Begin financial recovery and stability building
- Develop new social connections and activities
- Process emotions through therapy or support groups
- Avoid major life decisions during adjustment period

long-term Success Strategies:

- Continue personal growth and development
- Build wealth systematically, through strategic planning
- Maintain strong relationships with children
- Consider future relationship readiness carefully
- Share wisdom with other men facing similar challenges
- Create legacy of resilience and calculated decisions

EMERGENCY ACTION PLANS

If Served with Papers Unexpectedly:

1. Don't panic or react emotionally
2. Read everything carefully and completely
3. Contact attorney immediately (within 24–48 hours)
4. Don't sign anything without legal review
5. Begin immediate implementation of Four Pillars
6. Document the circumstances of service

If False Allegations Are Made:

1. Contact attorney immediately
2. Gather all evidence supporting your character
3. Compile witness list who can testify to your behavior
4. Avoid any contact with spouse except through attorney
5. Document your whereabouts and activities thoroughly
6. Follow all court orders precisely regardless of fairness

If Custody Is Threatened:

1. Continue normal parenting activities unless legally prohibited
2. Document all interactions with children meticulously
3. Maintain school and activity involvement visibly
4. Gather evidence of positive parenting and home environment
5. Request custody evaluation if appropriate
6. Consider temporary agreements to maintain access

STRATEGIC COMMUNICATION TEMPLATES

Professional Co-parenting Email Template:

"Subject: [Child's Name] - [Specific Topic]

Hello [Ex-spouse's name],

I'm writing regarding [specific child-related issue].
[State facts clearly and objectively]
I propose [specific solution or request].
Please let me know your thoughts by [specific date] so we can coordinate appropriately.

Thank you,
[Your name]"

Attorney Communication Guidelines:

- Always be honest and complete in your communications
- Provide documents and information promptly when requested
- Ask questions when you don't understand advice or strategy
- Communicate concerns about costs or timeline early
- Focus conversations on strategy rather than emotions
- Keep personal feelings about spouse separate from legal strategy

MONTHLY REVIEW CHECKLIST

Financial Progress:

- Review budget - actual vs. planned spending
- Assess progress toward emergency fund goals
- Monitor credit score and report changes
- Evaluate investment performance and contributions
- Plan for upcoming large expenses or obligations

Parenting Relationship:

- Assess quality of time spent with children
- Review any co-parenting challenges and solutions
- Plan for upcoming school events, activities, or schedule changes
- Consider children's changing needs and interests
- Document positive parenting moments and achievements

Personal Development:

- Evaluate physical health and fitness progress
- Assess emotional stability and stress management
- Review social connections and relationship quality
- Consider career advancement opportunities or changes
- Plan for personal interests and hobby development

Strategic Planning:

- Review long-term goals and progress toward achievement
- Assess any needed adjustments to strategies or timelines
- Plan for upcoming challenges or opportunities
- Consider professional guidance needs in any areas
- Update documentation and record-keeping systems

SUCCESS METRICS AND MILESTONES

6-Month Indicators:

- Stable co-parenting communication without regular conflict
- Financial stability with consistent budget management
- Established new routines and social connections
- Emotional regulation during challenging interactions
- Clear direction for long-term goals and plans

1-Year Indicators:

- Children comfortable and thriving in both homes
- Financial recovery showing measurable progress

- New identity and social life established
- Dating readiness assessment, if desired
- Ability to help others facing similar challenges

2-Year Indicators:

- Excellent co-parenting relationship with minimal friction
- Strong financial position with growing net worth
- Healthy romantic relationship, if desired
- Career advancement or business success
- Physical and mental health better than during marriage

5-Year Vision:

- Model of successful post-divorce transformation
- Strong relationships with adult/older children
- Financial independence and wealth building success
- Meaningful contribution to others through experience
- Life satisfaction exceeding pre-divorce levels

FINAL STRATEGIC REMINDERS

Documentation Saves Everything: When in doubt, document! Photos, emails, texts, and written records provide proof when memory fails and disputes arise.

Professional Guidance Pays: The cost of good legal, financial, and therapeutic advice is insignificant compared to the cost of mistakes or missed opportunities due to not seeking it.

Calculated Decisions Beat Emotional Reactions: Every decision should be evaluated based on long-term consequences rather than short-term satisfaction or vindication.

Your Children Watch Everything: How you handle this challenge teaches them how to handle their own life difficulties. Model the behavior and values you want them to adopt.

This Too Shall Pass: Divorce is temporary. The strategic decisions you make during this period are not. Choose wisely.

Growth Through Adversity: The skills, wisdom, and strength you develop from navigating divorce successfully will serve you in every future challenge and opportunity.

For Updated Resources and Additional Support:
Visit www.mensdivorcenetwork.com for current legal forms, strategy updates, and professional referrals in your area.

Legal Disclaimer: This appendix provides educational information only and does not constitute legal advice. Divorce laws vary by state and change frequently. Always consult with qualified professionals in your jurisdiction for guidance specific to your situation.

ACKNOWLEDGMENTS

Finishing this book has been a labor of love. It's been a journey of self-reflection, lessons learned, and a few mistakes along the way. More than anything, this book is my message to men everywhere: divorce isn't the end. It's a chance to start over — maybe for the first time in your life — with clarity, purpose, and strength.

To my husband, Rafael — my best friend and the person who reminds me every day what love is supposed to feel like. I didn't get it right the first time, but marrying you was the best decision I've ever made. Your patience, humor, and steady belief in me made this possible. To every man reading this who thinks divorce means the end of love — Rafael is living proof that your best relationship might be waiting on the other side. Sometimes you have to go through hell to find heaven.

To my daughter, Sydney, whose intelligence, wit, and heart make life brighter every single day. You keep me laughing, humble, and inspired.

To my parents, Ken and Dreka, thank you for everything — your love, your example, and the work ethic you built into me from the beginning. I'm grateful every day for the foundation you gave me.

To my brother, Josh, and my sister-in-law, Brittany, thank you for being my constant cheerleaders and for always showing up when it mattered most.

To my extended family — especially Carol, Richie, Twanna, Kimberly, and Max — thank you for challenging me, keeping me honest, and never letting me take myself too seriously. You've all shaped me in your own way.

To my past and present colleagues at New Jersey Divorce Solutions and now Netsquire, thank you for believing in what we're building. You've helped turn a simple idea — that divorce can be done with dignity, empathy, and strategy — into something that's changing lives. Christina Previte deserves her own line here — she helped me build something from nothing, believed in a better way to handle divorce when everyone said we were crazy, and had my back through it all.

To every man who sat in my office, feeling like his world was ending — you're the reason this book exists. You came in broken, angry, scared. But you taught me that real strength isn't about not breaking. It's about how you rebuild. Every lesson, every insight, every page comes from watching you transform from victims to victors. You taught me more about courage than any law book ever could. You trusted me with your darkest moments, and watching you come out the other side stronger? That's what keeps me doing this work.

To my friends and mentors, too many to mention individually — the ones who pushed me, questioned me, and told me the truth when I didn't want to hear it — thank you. You helped me find my voice and stay grounded while using it.

To every guest who joined me on the *Get Divorced Without Getting Screwed* podcast through Season 5 — thank you for showing up with honesty, vulnerability, and heart. The stories you told and the wisdom you shared became the backbone of this book. Whether you were a lawyer, therapist, coach, or someone brave enough to share your own experience, you helped start a conversation that men everywhere needed to hear. A huge thank you to each of you: Aaron Maltz, Adelaide Dow, Allyson Fusella, Ariel Peres, Bailey Heiser, Beverly Perryman, Brittany Racine, Brittney Phillips, Carrie Sackett, Christina Previte, Cody Jones, Dale Valor, Dorcy Pruter, Andrea Liner, Karen Molano, Kristen Strom, Eric Chilton, Hubert Johnson, Irslan Ali, James Bastian, James Brien, James Newberry, Janet Philbin, Jayden Aubryn, Jeff Landers, Jen Mitchell, Jennifer J. McCaskill, Jennifer Warren Medwin, Jeremy Davis, Jimmy Joseph, Jorge Vasquez, Judith Weigle, Katie Jordan, Kenneth Harrell, Kim Bowen, Kimberly Mansfield, Kristin M. Lis, Lauren Derick, Lee Povey, Melanie Verstraete, Michelle Sarao, Nancy Burger, Nancy Sawyer, Nanci Smith, Niomi Hurley, Paige Dempsey, Regie Tiu, The Dadvocate, Rose Clark, Sarah Armstrong, Sarah Jacobs, Scott Orr, Stephanie Ann, Stephanie Hunnell, Stephanie McPhail, Stephen A. Weisberg, Teresa Trieb, Tracy A. Malone, and Warren Lieff.

Each of you helped make this movement possible.

And finally, to every man who's ever sat across from me, feeling lost, angry, or scared — this book is for you. You might not have chosen to be here, but you get to decide what happens next. Divorce doesn't define you. It's your reset button. Use it.

Here's to second chances — to rebuilding, to freedom, and to the man you're becoming. Now stop reading the acknowledgments and start writing your comeback story. Your new life isn't going to build itself. It's time to get to work.

ABOUT THE AUTHOR

John Nachlinger knows what it's like to watch your life explode. He's lived through divorce himself — the confusion, the anger, the fear of what comes next. And he came out the other side determined to make sure other men never have to go through it the same way.

Now, as a New Jersey divorce attorney, mediator, and men's divorce strategist, John has helped thousands of men navigate divorce without losing everything that matters. Fed up with watching lawyers get rich while families got destroyed, he built something different — *Netsquire*, one of the first flat-fee divorce law firms in the country. His approach is simple: no hourly billing, no courtroom bloodbaths, just strategy, clarity, and peace.

John's straight-talk approach to divorce, relationships, and life has been featured in *Law.com*, *Newsweek*, *Parents Magazine*, the *New York Post*, *AP News*, *The Guardian*, and *HuffPost*. He's been a guest on numerous podcasts — including *Divorce, etc.*, *Mediate This!*, *Modern Divorce*, *Midlife Mix*, *Maximum Lawyer*, and *Better Divorce Academy* — as well as news outlets across the country, including ABC, FOX, and NPR affiliates.

Through his own hit podcast, *Get Divorced Without Getting Screwed*, John brings together attorneys, therapists, coaches, and everyday men to have the conversations the divorce industry avoids — real, raw, and necessary.

John believes most men lose in divorce not because they're weak, but because they're unprepared. This book changes that. It provides men with a playbook to protect their money, their children, and their sanity — and to rebuild their lives on their own terms.

He lives in New Jersey with his husband, Rafael, and their daughter, Sydney — living proof that there's life, and love, after divorce.